ADVANCE PRAISE

"No great business was built alone. You need a team to 10X your business, and TeamWork gives you the roadmap for scaling your team."

—GRANT CARDONE, REAL ESTATE MOGUL AND AUTHOR
OF THE NEW YORK TIMES BESTSELLER *THE 10X RULE*

"The culture of your organization is created either by design or default. In TeamWork, Natalie Dawson shares how to create a culture by design so you can attract the right fabulous people, create an exciting work environment, and build an incredible company. Business truly is a team sport. Natalie shows you how to create the right team!"

—SHARON LECHTER, CO-AUTHOR OF NEW YORK TIMES
BESTSELLERS *RICH DAD POOR DAD* AND *EXIT RICH*

"TeamWork takes the guesswork out of building a great team."

—JIM TREVLING, CO-OWNER OF BOSTON'S
PIZZA AND STAR OF DRAGON'S DEN

"TeamWork is a must-read for all leaders who want to create a winning culture."

—PAUL WILLE, CHIEF OPERATING OFFICER
AT WUNDERMAN THOMPSON

TEAM/WORK

HOW TO BUILD A HIGH-PERFORMANCE TEAM

NATALIE DAWSON

HOUNDSTOOTH
PRESS

TEAMWORK

How to Build a High-Performance Team

ISBN   978-1-5445-2558-7   *Hardcover*
        978-1-5445-2557-0   *Paperback*
        978-1-5445-2556-3   *Ebook*

To Brandon—the most remarkable leader, partner, and mentor. Thank you for always believing in me and showing me the way.

CONTENTS

INTRODUCTION

I am an expert at leading teams and developing people; my goal is to make you an expert too. And in a fraction of the time it took me.

I've dedicated the last decade of my career to understanding how to align team members' goals to the business goals in order to create a culture where everyone is winning. I've led my own teams and worked with over one thousand clients to help them create high-performance teams. Building and scaling teams is my passion. Over the past two years, I've been responsible for the hiring, training, firing, and operating at an organization called Cardone Ventures. In our first full year in business, we generated $16.4 million in annual revenue. I'm currently writing this in July of our second year of business, and we're on track to hit $40 million in annual revenue. We currently have sixty-six team members and will end the year at eighty.

Why is this important?

I need you to know that the tools I'm going to introduce to you in this book *actually* work in real business. They are real, proven, tangible processes and concepts that I have actually applied. This book is not about theory. I'm not going to tell you what I *think* you should do—I'm going to share with you what I did and why it worked. I don't do fluff. We're going to dive right into the nitty gritty because, in my experience, authors tend to confuse readers with their long stories and roundabout points. Business owners today need the tools to implement into their businesses tomorrow to get a better result. And that's what I'm here to give you. Results.

I'm also going to share with you the successes our clients have had by implementing these same principles. That way, you know it's not just Cardone Ventures that's had real results using these tools. Everything in this book is structured so you get out of Lalaland about "how to be a better boss" and what a "strong culture really looks like." There are thousands of ideas all over the internet about how company happy hours, sleep pods, and free food are what drive culture. That might work at Google *today*, but I'm interested in helping your small business drive true culture through operational and financial efficiencies.

The reality is that most businesses fail. We've all heard the stats: 20 percent of businesses fail within the first year, and half of them have gone out of business by the fifth year. Being an entre- preneur and growing a business might seem cool and trendy on social media, but it's something only few actually make work. I think a more telling set of stats is the breakpoints of businesses when it comes to their people. Did you know that out of 31.5 million small- to mid-sized businesses in the US, 25 million only have one employee, the founder? Another 5.3 million have two to fifteen employees, and only six hundred thousand US businesses have more than fifteen employees.

What does this mean? Creating a business through people is one of the most difficult things you can do. Growing and scaling a team might sound easy in theory, but actually doing it means you've beat the odds. So that's exactly what this book is going to give you: the whole system it takes to create a people process within your business, including the resources and structure you need to create cultural, operational, and financial scale. This is the definition of TeamWork.

66/99

CHAPTER 1

EMPLOYEE ENGAGEMENT CYCLE

YOUR TEAM IS STUCK

I hate to be the bearer of bad news, but you didn't buy this book for me to lie to you. Your team is stuck.

The number one question I get asked when speaking to hundreds of business owners is, "How do I motivate my people?" Others chime in with agreeing sentiments:

- "No one works as hard as me."
- "My team is happy with their nine-to-five."
- "I can't find any great people."
- "This new generation is entitled and lazy."
- "People don't work as hard as they used to."

If you've thought any of these things about your team, stop being a victim and start playing offense. The employee engagement cycle is going to be the tool we use to identify where your team members are in their roles at your organization. The first phase is employee alignment, the second phase is employee development, and the third phase is employee transition. These three phases pinpoint what part of the growth cycle your team members are in, at any given point in their career with you.

EMPLOYEE MANAGEMENT CYCLE

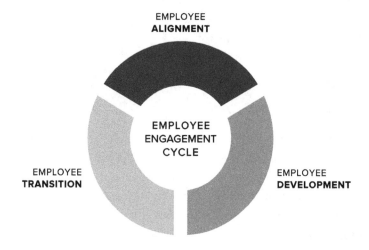

Setting relationships with your team members up for success through the interview and onboarding process is low-hanging fruit. We will dive into how to optimize your existing processes. But the greatest opportunity I see time and again is the lack of emphasis on what skills team members need to develop to be able to transition into a new role. Instead, most, if not all, of your team members are stuck in a perpetual state of development.

Let's think about your onboarding process. Unless you've painted a massive picture for them that they have an opportunity to move from their current role to being promoted to a senior and then to leading a team, your team member is perpetually stuck in the development phase. I think of this as employee purgatory. If you're not showing them a big picture of your business growth and how they can contribute, they will never know what the next step looks like. They don't understand what skills they need to develop because they don't know why they would need to develop into something different; the picture has not been created.

So when you think about this model, identify which bucket each of your existing team members is in. Are they in alignment, development, or transition? If they're in alignment, they've either just been hired within the past ninety days, or they were just promoted within the last ninety days.

Depending on your growth, you should target 20 percent of your team to be in the alignment category. You should target 60 percent of your team to be in the development phase, which means that they are focused on being a top performer in their role. They are working on themselves, working on their goals, and adding skillsets to their ability to contribute. They're doing their job and ideally being the best at their job.

But the reason that you can inspire people to be the best at their job isn't so that they can just be a top performer and stay there for the rest of their lives. The next game for them is figuring out how to transition. But here's the deal: they're only allowed to transition if they are the best. So it is okay that people stay in the development phase the longest amount of time because adding valuable skillsets doesn't happen in a weekend. But remember this: the only reason that they stay in there *and* push themselves to be the best is because they're able to see a picture for what transition looks like. When it comes to the transition phase, you should target 20 percent of your team.

Let's put our team member hat on: I've been an account manager for eighteen months, but the reason I am striving to be the absolute best account manager possible is because I understand that the next opportunity is for me to be a senior account manager, and a senior account manager looks like additional pay, looks like additional responsibilities because I've demonstrated in my current role that I'm able to add more value. So once I've moved through development and have officially transitioned into the senior account manager role, what happens next? I'm back in alignment!

Once a team member has started with an organization, gone through the development phase, and successfully transitioned up into a new role and new responsibilities because they added value not only to themselves but to the organization, they then go back into alignment because they are in a new role with a new position and a new set of responsibilities. In any new role, a team member has to realign. How does this role impact the organization's Mission, Vision, and Core Values? What is the job description that details what would make them a top performer? What development is needed to fill and succeed at this new role? How does this role align with and contribute to the organization's goals?

The goal with every team member in your organization is for them to do this over and over again: align, develop, transition into a new role *because the business is growing* to align, develop, transition into their next role *because the business is growing*, which then allows them again to align, develop, transition. In the example of the account manager, they now have to become the best at being a senior account manager so they can go through a transition because now, instead of being a senior account manager, they're able to be the director over all of the account managers. This cycle should continue and continue and continue to grow and evolve over time because those team members are adding more value. Eventually this account manager has an opportunity to become a vice president and future partner of the organization.

HOW TO GET YOUR TEAM UNSTUCK

These are the only reasons team members get stuck:

1. They don't want to grow.
2. The business isn't growing.
3. They aren't achieving results.

Luckily there is a solution, and it's found in reengineering your people process. Even if you never said, "There's no opportunity for growth here" to your team, devoid of communication and a structure that moves team members through a growth cycle, that's still what they're experiencing: no growth. If *they* don't see growth opportunity, who is going to help you grow? This is the fallacy in small business today: you can't do it alone, nor should you. You team can and should be creating growth in your organization, but if they don't see that, it's entirely up to you. No one is coming to save you and your business. There's no business fairy godmother that is magically going to gift you the client pipeline of your dreams. She's not going to whisk away top talent from your competitors and deliver them to your doorstep.

But the good news is, you don't need a fairy godmother. You just need a people process that systematically takes a team member through the employee engagement cycle and continues to cycle them through it. Your attention on that will make you your own damn fairy godmother.

It's not your team's fault that they're stuck. All problems in your organization are created by you—your people problems included. Your people problems are your fault. But before we can determine if you have a handful of team members on your team who actually are problematic (those people do exist), you have to implement a people process.

In this book, I am going to break down each of the components required to build your people process and give you the tools and tips I've learned over the past eight years so that it won't take you as long as it took me. Things to keep in mind:

Every piece is important. The people process is built as a system, and all of the parts are necessary for it to work. If you pick and choose what you're going to implement, your system will be incomplete and there will be natural consequences.

Keep the big picture in mind. Being in the people business is fraught with challenges. You will need to constantly gauge the pulse of the organization and be aware of issues that can pull you off target. But your attention to this is for one purpose: to grow and scale your business. When you're feeling overwhelmed with the amount of work or frustrated with team members who are underperforming, remember to keep the end goal in mind. You will never hire the perfect team or grow a business to not have problems. That's not the goal. The goal is to make an impact in your business through serving your clients and creating financial freedom for you, your family, your team members, and hopefully many generations to come. With this in mind, you'll be able to move through the problems you encounter swiftly because it's all part of getting to where you want to go.

EMPLOYEE ALIGNMENT

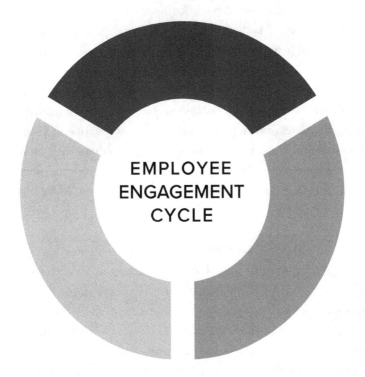

EMPLOYEE
ALIGNMENT

EMPLOYEE
ENGAGEMENT
CYCLE

The baseline for aligning brand new team members with your organization is having a clear Mission statement, Vision statement, and Core Values. These elements work in tandem and should be inescapable for your team. They should guide your hiring, rewarding, and firing process and give any new team member a crystal-clear understanding of the most vital information about your organization: why you exist, where you are going, and how the culture is defined.

Once there is a baseline understanding of why the business exists and where it's going, the next piece of the alignment phase is the interview process. This is one of the most critical and overlooked touchpoints. Do you currently use the same interview questions for every candidate? Are you selling them or are they selling you? What information do you put on your recruitment sites? Is there a page on your website specifically for potential team members? The interview process and information that's available about your company is oftentimes the biggest area of opportunity for business owners. The reason this step is so important is because *you* need to have confidence in it. To the extent that you don't have confidence in your ability to attract the right employees and align them with your organization, you will allow bad behavior from your existing team members and be unwilling to get rid of them. More on that in Chapter 16.

The final component of the alignment phase is the job descriptions. Job descriptions should set the expectations for each role as to the objectives, competencies, and metrics required. Clear and well-thought-out job descriptions define the value that every role plays in the organization. Without well-organized job descriptions, you will find chaos in your environment. It might work while you're small, but as your organization grows, it's important that every role knows what they're responsible for and what someone else is responsible for. Business communication and processes get complex as you add more people to the mix. And remember this: the less chaos in your environment, the more confidence you'll have to expand.

EMPLOYEE DEVELOPMENT

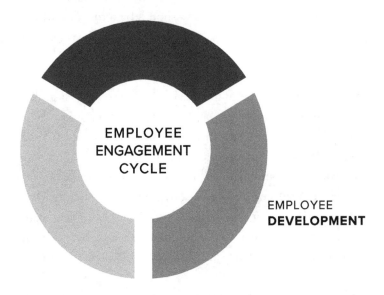

In the development phase, one of the biggest areas of opportunity is the onboarding process. If you don't have a clear onboarding process, you're going to find that even with the perfect interview process, you can lose great team members or turn them into underperformers because they don't actually know what they're supposed to do, how they're supposed to do it, or the results they need to achieve.

If you don't have huge expansion plans, this isn't the first place you should focus, but if you do, get surgical about every step in this process and get in front of it now. I can promise you: this process is rocket fuel and sets you up for success for having new team members be great contributors immediately. Or it's going to be the reason you had big goals but broke down at takeoff because the internal system combusted.

Another tool in the development phase is the daily all-team meeting. These set the tone instantly. A team member's first fifteen minutes on their first day should be a meeting where the entire team is present. As a brand new employee, seeing the energy, hearing how you operate, and experiencing the professionalism and speed creates a true example of your expectation of how the culture performs. Are you guys fast? Are you organized? Are there wins? Are you guys reporting data? Are things organized, or is there a lot of work that needs to be done? Your ability to put culture into that meeting is also a way that you're aligning team members to these priorities. Every day, you're constantly going back to the main thing instead of getting distracted or potentially having that brand new team member you've onboarded get confused as to where they fit into the organization.

Employee handbooks are one of the most unsexy, not fun things to create for your organization; however, your employee handbook is the bedrock for being able to create clarity, understanding, and alignment. When a new team member is coming on board with a robust handbook, it's not going to fix every problem that you have, but it gives you a place to share what every person needs to know to be set up for success. It should detail the policies, rules, and expectations and, more importantly, what happens when these things are disregarded.

I'm going to dive into a number of other tools, like personal, professional, and financial goal planning, organizational charts, and quarterly team meetings, but I don't want to spoil all the fun.

EMPLOYEE TRANSITION

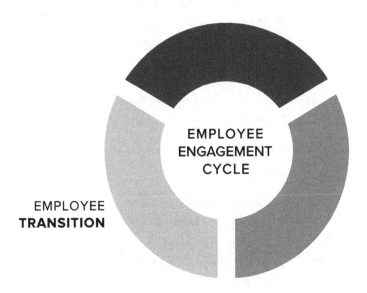

EMPLOYEE ENGAGEMENT CYCLE

EMPLOYEE TRANSITION

Transition is the goal for each of your team members. But before we dive into the transition phase, I want to clarify that there are two types of transition: up or out.

The tools I cover in the transition section cover both scenarios because both need to happen. If you're a business owner who has had the same team for eight years but want to triple your revenue, the reality is you will need new people to help you get there. The people you have now certainly contributed to getting to where you are, but your goals have changed and the people who got you here are rarely the same people who will get you where you want to go. That's not to say that all of them won't still be with you. Some of them will be in for the ride. But as your business goals get bigger, I can assure you that everyone won't want to take the ride. And that's okay. But when it's clear that they don't want to be on the ride, it's your responsibility to get them off, not have them scream, kick, and yell the entire time just to distract and demotivate the other enthused riders.

On the other hand, the transition up process should be laid out and clearly articulated to every team member. Many organizations call this career pathing or succession planning. I refer to this as the Employee Maturity Model. This model gives everyone the opportunity to understand what it takes to get a promotion and what pay is associated with each role. This starts at a coordinator and moves up to manager, senior manager, director, senior director, vice president, senior vice president, executive vice president, and C-Suite. Each role should have identified competencies that indicate when someone is ready to be considered for a promotion. It's objective-, competency-, and metrics-driven to align all components together that will create financial impact and overall value to the organization.

Are you ready to build a team that actually *works*?

EMPLOYEE **ALIGNMENT**

- ☑ **MISSION**
- ☐ VISION
- ☐ CORE VALUES
- ☐ WHERE TO USE THEM
- ☐ JOB POST
- ☐ INTERVIEW PROCESS

66/99

CHAPTER 2

MISSION STATEMENT

I started my career when I was twenty years old. I was an economics major at a private college in the Pacific Northwest and had no real interest in starting my career. I was about to start my junior year and was looking forward to spending my summer like I had the years prior: volunteering. At that time, I was incredibly involved in a number of volunteer organizations that served the growing homeless community in downtown Portland. We would pass out lunches, help people get jobs, and provide them a space for judgment-free conversations that led to friendships. The last thing I wanted to do was make money, but my parents had different plans for me.

After a particularly challenging finals week had wrapped up, I was enjoying my first week of summer break when I picked up a call from my mom that changed the trajectory of my life. Like most life-changing moments, I didn't realize it while it was happening. It was an average cloudy June day, and she informed me that she had secured an internship for me that started the coming Monday. I put up a fight initially but didn't have much of a choice. My livelihood, car insurance, meals, and gas money for my '93 Buick Century depended on it, so "no" was not an answer.

For the next three days, I dreaded the upcoming start date and soaked in my last few hours of freedom before starting work. When Monday rolled around, I was less than enthused and already longed to have my summer back. The company I was interning at was located in a red brick building that looked corporate and stiff. As soon as I walked in the building and felt the chill of the overcirculated air, my dread turned to irritation. Everyone was dressed professionally, including myself, but no one seemed to know where I was going to sit. They hadn't planned on having an intern, and the building was filled to the brim, so they made a makeshift workstation for me right next to the elevator on the third floor.

What I didn't realize at the time is the third floor was the place to be. The executive wing was on one side of the building with the HR, Accounting, and Finance departments on the other. I didn't know what any of that meant at the time, but it was certainly foreshadowing where my career was headed.

After the desk debacle was situated, I spent the rest of my first day at my new job watching training videos and started reading the stack of leadership books I had been issued. Spending my afternoon reading was surprisingly delightful, and I began to think this whole internship thing wasn't going to be so bad. This was the first time I had ever held a job, and I very much looked forward to collecting my $8.33 per hour paycheck the following week.

The second day at my new internship held a surprise. It started off with picking up my reading from the day before. After three hours, I got up from my awkwardly positioned desk to head to the restroom when the president of the company passed me in the hallway. "Hey, Natalie!" he said, as he swiftly passed by. "What's our Mission statement?" Only then did he turn around and stop so he could hear my response.

I froze. I didn't know what the answer was. And I hated how that felt. Today, I pride myself on preparation and learning just about everything I possibly can about a business, but on this particular day eight years ago, I found myself in a situation without the ammunition I needed to properly answer the president's question, and I admitted as much to him. I told him, "I'm not sure, but I'm very interested to learn about it!" in a high-pitched tone to mask my nervousness and lack of interest. He then said to me words I will never forget: "Nobody is allowed to be a leech in our environment. You are here because you serve a purpose. Random people doing random things who don't know why they're here do not belong to this organization."

Some people might think that was harsh. It was shocking, but in that moment, he was defining and protecting the culture. This is every leader's job. As a new team member, I needed to figure out why I was there and what I was going to contribute. This moment shifted my awareness about why team members are actually added: they're responsible to contribute. But if *they* don't know why they're there, how are they supposed to add value to your clients and team?

I find that most business owners do not set this as a standard in their environment because they assume that everyone knows what they know. This couldn't be further from the truth. Without a clear Mission (and a process to ensure everyone on your team knows it), you will build an environment of leeches who randomly do things that don't contribute to where you want to go. Then you'll sit back and be victimized by your team and say stupid things like, "I can't find any great people in my market."

Don't be a victim of your lack of discipline in your culture. The starting point in any business is a clearly defined Mission statement.

THE MISSION = THE WHY

In the simplest of terms, your Mission statement is your why. Your Mission statement should succinctly be able to answer the question: why does my company exist?

This statement should be the heartbeat behind why you and your team have decided to show up to work each and every day. It allows your team to understand why it is that you exist. Think of your Mission statement as a filter. This filter helps define the quality of the environment that you're working to create. A focused Mission statement eliminates the friction that makes business hard.

You see, when you don't have your why in place, business can get really hard. As a business owner, you're making decisions that affect the trajectory of your business every day. When you're making decisions with your Mission in mind—a Mission that is oriented around serving your customers—making those tough decisions is that much easier. Less friction. More action. More accountability. Better results. And isn't that ultimately what you want?

CLIENTS vs TEAM MEMBERS

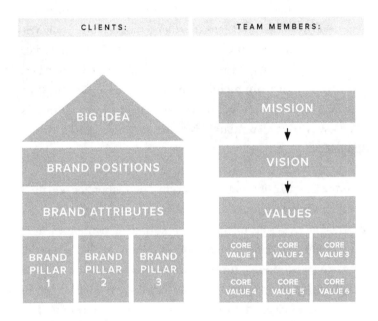

It's easy to get hung up on your Mission statement because most people are confused about who they are talking to with their Mission statement. For the purposes of this book, the audience for your Mission statement is your *team*, and the audience for your Brand statement is your *clients*. The reason there are two statements is because you're talking to two separate people: one person you're looking to hire and join your team and the other you're looking to buy from you. Your business needs *both* to grow. Clients I've worked with try to make one statement for both groups, and I don't recommend this. One statement as a catch-all won't be effective.

MISSION STATEMENT = TEAM

You didn't get in business so that you can have a job for the rest of your life. You got in business to build something great. When you first started, you likely had dreams of hiring teams of people who are high performers and work collaboratively. This doesn't have to be a dream. Any business has the potential to scale with teams of people, but you have to recognize that you need to market to them in order to find them. Your Mission statement is a critical element of the marketing materials you will need to create to attract top talent. Just like your best customers, your team members need to understand your business, but from a slightly different angle than your customers. That's why we differentiate a Mission statement and a Brand statement.

A compelling Mission statement sets the foundation for potential team members to understand if they align with your business. If your business sells furniture to first-time apartment owners, your Mission statement might sound something like: we transform our customers' empty apartments into homes through custom designs and budget-friendly furniture. With this Mission statement, it's clear that your goal is to help your customer feel at home in their space. You can attract top design and sales talent through sharing that your designs are custom, which is a differentiator in that market since not all furniture stores even offer design. It also makes it clear that the customer experience is important to you. If it's important to you, it needs to be clearly communicated in your Mission so you can hold team members accountable to this standard when they fall short. And trust me, they will.

BRAND STATEMENT = CLIENTS

The Brand statement is aimed to resonate and connect with prospective clients. I'm no marketing expert but can succinctly sum up that the Brand statement should be directed toward grabbing the mindshare and speaking the language of the target client you'd like to do business with. Let's say your furniture store's target client is a twenty- to thirty-year-old male who is looking to buy new furniture for his first adult apartment. Your website, social pages, and places where you advertise to grab his attention will be different from the places you target the team members you are looking to attract to grow your existing furniture business and scale to add ten locations in your market. The above Mission statement would be on a careers page, whereas every brand touchpoint where you're speaking to a client is filtered through your Brand statement.

CRITERIA

Let's get into the nitty gritty. I told you I would give you the tools, and all of the Mission statement magic is in the criteria below. These criteria can be used to evaluate your current Mission statement to see if it's going to work as a key element of your Employee Engagement Cycle. If you don't have a current Mission statement, that is not a problem. Use these criteria as a guide as you craft yours.

DOES YOUR MISSION PINPOINT YOUR "WHY"?

This statement should define why your business exists. Who do you serve? What impact does the organization make? Only you as the business owner can answer this question. You started your business to do...what? There should be no question about what it is your business exists to do. This isn't philosophical.

It's a tangible impact that makes your future team members think, "Wow—I want to help with THAT." Note that the Mission statement should have nothing to do with you or your team—your Mission is about your *clients*. We'll get into why this is important, but take heed of this now. It will make all the difference when you have underperforming team members.

CAN YOU ANSWER "HOW"?

No one likes a bullshitter. This is a critical question to consider before you start shouting your why to the world. Here's the deal: it's okay not to have every step mapped out in order to achieve your Mission, but you can't sound like an idiot either. Your Mission statement should create confidence in your team, but if it's so far out there and you aren't able to tie out your product or service growth to your why, you need to either spend time creating a plan (this is ALWAYS preferred) or you need to dial your Mission back. I've worked with clients who have these massive Mission statements but look perplexed when you ask them, "How are you going to get there?" When someone asks you, be able to have a sixty-to-ninety-second response on how you achieve the Mission you've stated—you don't have to pull out an eighty-seven-page business plan.

IS IT ONE SENTENCE?

Make it short. No longer than one sentence, please. This can be challenging because you do *so* many things, but let's go back to why you're creating this in the first place: it's for you and your team to be able to rattle off with ease when talking with a candidate or when you're refocusing a team member on the main thing instead of getting distracted with a shiny, out-of-scope idea. If your current Mission statement is a paragraph, move that sucker over to your website as a description of what you do and condense your actual Mission statement to one sentence.

DOES IT START WITH A "WE" PLUS A VERB?

This is an easy one: start your Mission statement with "We" and then a verb. Great verbs include the following: transform, create, help, change, impact, etc. So your statement would read like this: "ABC Company transforms how _____."

This format creates clarity on the impact your company creates, feels aspirational, and serves as an invitation to others who are passionate about your why as well. Remember: you are looking for people who are just as passionate as you are about your cause, but it's *your* job to make your passion and intent clear to them.

IS IT EASY TO MEMORIZE?

It shouldn't take more than a day for a new team member to memorize your Mission statement. Think about running into your newest team member on their second day of work; they should be able to state your Mission with confidence and clarity. If it takes longer than that, your Mission statement is likely too complicated or long. You should be able to state it with zero hesitation. When I work with clients during a workshop, I'll ask them for their Mission statement, and they'll pull up their website to read it to me. Flunk. Fail. Nope. This doesn't work. Remove some words, and let's do this again. You can't expect your team to know something that you don't, especially as it pertains to your why.

IS IT WRITTEN IN PLAINSPOKEN LANGUAGE?

No corporate jargon or big fancy words allowed. The more

fancy the word is, the less likely somebody is going to be able to actually remember what your Mission statement is. And you need them to remember it. You need them to feel impacted by it. You are not trying to confuse people. Early in my career, I remember attending networking events where people would talk in such high-level terms about what they did. I would leave those conversations entirely confused and unclear about what they were saying, but I didn't ask because I didn't want to look stupid. I would nod my head like I understood. *This* is why you don't put industry speak or fluff into your Mission. The point isn't to confuse people—it's to bring people into your environment who want to *help* you scale and grow your business. No one wants to work at a place where they're confused by what the company does. If they don't understand what you do, you're not going to be able to get them in the door.

IS IT COMPELLING?

Create something that inspires and excites. I won't get all woo-woo on you here, but here's the deal: high performers don't just want to work hard and grind—they want to make a difference. If your Mission statement isn't compelling, why are you thinking it's going to attract top talent? This is more of a gut check than anything else. Read your existing Mission statement and ask: does this inspire me to get out of bed every morning? As the business owner, if you aren't compelled by your why, neither are your team or potential candidates. The reason behind the work you do should invigorate you.

I was working with a client on his Mission statement a few months ago, and when we got to this criterion, he said, "I struggle with this because my current Mission doesn't really excite me. I read it, and they are nice words, but I don't feel anything." If you feel this way, you have two options: update your Mission statement to something that *does* compel you or refocus your business on something you truly want to impact. If you aren't fulfilled by the impact of the business you're creating, or if it's unethical, make a change. You will never find great people if you don't believe in the work you're doing.

Now that you have the criteria, take fifteen minutes and draft or update your Mission statement. Don't overthink it! So many people get all philosophical and heady with this conversation. This is not a time to question your life's existence. Just think about the business's why and fill in the blank: "My business exists to serve _____." It doesn't have to be perfect, and you shouldn't spend months belaboring it. Don't move off of this chapter until you have a solid statement.

AT CARDONE VENTURES

Our Mission statement is vital to the work we do at Cardone Ventures because it *literally* guides the way we do business: we help our clients achieve their personal, professional, and financial goals through the growth of their businesses.

It's simple, it's actionable, and it's applicable to everyone in the business. It's clear in the hiring and onboarding process that each and every decision we make hinges on whether its outcome will support our client's business growth. When a new idea is shared, we run it through this filter. When a team member is wasting time complaining, we use it to refocus on why we're all here: to help business owners. A strong Mission statement has the ability to refocus any negative or misaligned team member to the main thing: serving your clients and creating an impact. We'll get into how to use this in a corrective conversation with a team member in Chapter 15.

The whole idea behind this is to be able to create confidence in the people that you are going to need on your team in order for them to understand how they're going to align with this Mission and be able to help you take the business to where you want it to go. But where is that exactly?

CLIENT EXAMPLES

"We transform the medical paradigm in our community through our focus on function, empowerment of our patients, and helping our patients achieve true health and wellness."

—BALANCE WELLSPACE

"We create an amazing experience for every patient."

—FLAWLESS DENTISTRY

"We transform real estate agents' lives through developing teams with multiple streams of income and creating generational wealth."

—THE SIMPLE LIFE

"We help people gain financial freedom by eliminating their tax liability."

—AERO & MARINE TAX PROFESSIONALS

"We deliver natural health products and education that helps people provide optimal care to themselves and their animals."

—SILVER LINING HERBS

"We provide state-of-the-art heating, cooling, and automation solutions that offer reliable comfort to the customers we serve."

—INLAND MECHANICAL SERVICE

EMPLOYEE **ALIGNMENT**

- ☑ MISSION
- ☑ **VISION**
- ☐ CORE VALUES
- ☐ WHERE TO USE THEM
- ☐ JOB POST
- ☐ INTERVIEW PROCESS

66 99

CHAPTER 3

VISION STATEMENT

Imagine this: you're in love. You've just met the person you want to spend the rest of your life with. The first few months are so amazing that you decide to tie the knot. Everything is pure bliss until the week following your honeymoon when you excitedly bring up the prospect of starting a family. Instead of the response you were expecting, you discover that she has no desire to have children for the next ten years. She wants to build her career and stay living in the city. The conversation gets heated because you vaguely remember discussing kids on one of your first dates but didn't press into the timing. You're also upset because you have hated living in the city for the past eight years as the traffic, people, and grind no longer carry the luster they did in your youth. You had already been looking at homes ninety minutes outside the city where you could have land and start raising a family.

Uh-oh. There's trouble in paradise.

Devoid of a clear Vision statement, this is exactly what is happening in your interview process. You're assessing technical and interpersonal skills of your team-member-to-be while entirely missing what the context of the conversation should be: where are you going and how can they help?

Assessing a candidate's aptitude based on today's business needs is only part of the equation. More than skill, you are looking for the willingness and alignment to go toward your target. You are not just looking for *any* team member. You are committed to making your Vision a reality, and you need team members to come alongside you and build with you.

You are looking for your brand of crazy. You can't assume that the people you interview are going to join your organization and be as excited as you are about solving big problems if you don't tell them ahead of time that's what you're looking for. You want them to be with you and the organization for the long run, to solve the big problems that must be overcome to hit the goals that you have. You need to have such clarity and singular focus on attracting the type of people who are your brand of crazy, who like to solve problems and want to push further.

The one thing I can promise you is they are out there. They aren't *everyone*, but they do exist. Finding extraordinary people is certainly more difficult than saying yes to any Joe Schmo who can merely do the job, but remember, *you're* in this to create something extraordinary. This is where you go back to your Mission statement. If you truly believe you can and will make an impact, you need to keep your eyes wide open to find people who want to do the same. I've interviewed hundreds and hundreds of team members. Only a small percentage get the opportunity to work with us because we're only looking for the best, the committed, the hungry, and the willing. Sometimes it's like finding a needle in a haystack. Well…it might not be as difficult as literally finding a needle in a haystack, but it is something that you have to put particular attention into when you're in the interview process. And so with that, let's dive into where exactly that is.

THE VISION = THE "WHERE"

It's easy to get caught up in day-to-day tasks—the hamster wheel of "just good enough"—that you never actually move the business forward. I know how frustrating it can be when you are putting the hours in just to get by and barely hit the same numbers you hit the year before. With a clear Vision, you should be able to use it as your guide for how you're spending your time, who you're investing in, and the big picture pieces you need to put together in order to actually achieve growth. The ultimate antidote to stagnation is through developing, communicating, and acting on a clear Vision.

Remember, your Vision's purpose is to describe what you want to achieve in the long run for your organization. These are the crucial considerations for developing an effective Vision:

- The Vision is designed to describe the long-term target for the organization.
  - Without a target, what is guiding day-to-day activities and strategic planning? If you don't know that you want to impact one thousand people, how will you organize the business's resources? Let me tell you: chaotically. Devoid of a clear Vision, you will chase "good" ideas and lose focus on the main thing. As a leader, it is your job to set the direction and continuously point back to it.
- The long-term change resulting from your work should be clear and inspirational.

- Again, clarity is crucial. As is conveying something your team can rally around, aspire to, and be inspired by. If where you're going doesn't excite you, you need to think bigger so that you put the energy behind what it's going to take to achieve your goals. As Grant Cardone's *The 10X Rule* states, start thinking 10X today so you'll take 10X action.
- Your Vision is a tool you must use to lead your group or organization to achieve quality results.
  - Yes, this is aspirational, but it's also operational. What will you achieve in the next ten years? Why does this matter? Because the Vision of your business is not a time for, "Yeah, but what about….?"-type thinking. You're distracting yourself from creating the best possible version of your business. This is your legacy. This is your moonshot. Let's get the team organized and start executing!

WHY WOULDN'T YOU CREATE A VISION STATEMENT?

It's important to address why you *wouldn't* have a Vision statement because it's my responsibility to sell you on implementing every single component inside this book. After working with over a thousand business owners, I've found that the primary hesitation behind not solidifying and sharing a Vision statement is self-doubt. This conversation typically sounds like this: "I know we can achieve X, but what if we don't? Then I've put it out there for our team and clients and failed." If you're feeling this way, you're not alone.

This is a normal feeling. It's the same reason that very few people share their goals. They don't want the accountability. They have uncertainty in themselves and their business opportunity. They don't want to publicly fail. They *think* they have what it takes, but what if they're wrong? When you build a business on self-doubt, I have certainty that either (a) it will take you longer than it needed to for you to get there, or (b) you'll never get there. Let's unpack both.

ADDING TIME

Confidence is magnetizing and the name of the building-a-high-performance-team game. High-performing team members will naturally choose opportunities that are in alignment with their capabilities. If you talk to your first prospective team member about what you "might" do and where the business "could" go without confidence and structure, the right person will opt out and the wrong person will take the job. When you're not confident in where you're going, you're not going to attract the people who can actually help you, and when you hire sub-performing talent, it requires more of your time, energy, and resources to create financial momentum in your business. You officially become a babysitter when you hire incapable talent, and the last thing you need when your business is growing is to clean up someone else's shit. You need to handle your appearance of lack of confidence through a strong, well-thought-out Vision statement that separates you from all of the other promising opportunities high performers have.

FAILING

"Failure is not an option" is only an applicable statement for people who won't quit. You're not going to quit on yourself, are you? Okay, good. So why even think twice about sharing your Vision statement? By setting and sharing your Vision, you are putting your fears to the side and declaring to your team, but most importantly yourself, that failure is not an option.

THREE VISION STATEMENTS

Now that you're in the right mindset for creating a clear, action-able Vision, I'm going to push you even further—you need three distinct Vision statements. One Vision statement for your brand, one for your people, and one for your revenue.

Why have three versions? You are looking for an array of team members to join you in taking the hill, and you need to account for the fact that people aren't all motivated by the same things. Some will be compelled by the brand, others the people, and a small group the financial impact. These are crucial elements of your organization, and this creates even more clarity about where your business is going in the next ten years.

Growth comes with challenges, and you are looking for people who get excited about solving the same problems you do. Saying "ABC company wants to be the best" is a nice Vision for some-one who takes things at face value. But to get to where you want to go, you need to start assimilating a rock star group of team members who are specifically driven to achieve a result, so let's break the Vision statements down.

BRAND: LEGACY AND IMPACT VISION STATEMENT

What is the quantifiable impact you are looking to make in the lives of your clients, patients, or customers? *This* is your Brand Vision statement. Your brand ultimately defines legacy and communicates its impact. Don't treat it as though it's out of your control. Use your Brand Vision statement to intentionally direct the overall impact the business will create and the legacy you want to build over the next ten years.

PEOPLE: CULTURE AND TEAM VISION STATEMENT

It's simply a fact: businesses don't move people—people move businesses. To move the business in the direction you want it to go, you need a clear, team-centric Vision to guide your people. The People Vision statement should share the goal for the type of culture and team alignment you're targeting.

REVENUE: FINANCIAL VISION STATEMENT

Businesses are created to solve problems and generate wealth. Therefore, there shouldn't be anything mysterious about your Financial Vision. Do you know your ten-year financial goal? If not, set the intention, and take the action. If your team is "not interested" in money, we need to take a step back. Just remember: you are interdependent on the people you've chosen to help you hit your goals. If they aren't serious about changing their own financial condition, why do you expect them to help you with yours?

Vision statements can be hard to develop because you likely started your business because you wanted to move *away* from something—a bad boss, dead-end job, etc. But how you got into business ownership is irrelevant because now your focus needs to shift to what you're *creating*. To truly create an impact, your goals and team will require long-term, strategic thinking and a clear decision: where are you going?

VISION CRITERIA
DOES IT ESTABLISH A TEN-YEAR OUTLOOK?

The Vision is not five years; it's not three years. We are saying ten years from now, what are we doing? Consultants debate about the timing around this, and you've likely heard different approaches. Why do I choose ten years? Ten years is far enough out that you don't have to have the mechanics figured out, but you can still put a plan in place to hit an aspirational target. It is far out enough to work toward. But it's not too close like five years. Can you have transparency into ten years? No, absolutely not. Five years is far out, but it's still too close to really make a monumental change and allow people to dream about what that could look like and what their impact could be.

Think of who you were ten years ago. I'm certain that everything in your life has changed and there have been things that ended up different than what you had planned or expected. The magnitude of what you can create over the next ten years is limitless. That is the spirit you want to harness when picking this target. What could you create over the next ten years? Let's put a stake in the ground.

IS IT QUANTIFIABLE?

I've gotten myself in a number of debates with clients who think "We will dominate our market" is a great Vision statement. As much as I love a good ole testosterone-filled Vision statement, my one question is "How will you know when that's actually happened?" There's not a clear point in time where anyone can definitively say that "domination" has occurred. This criterion is used to separate the serious business builders from the dreamers. Your Vision should have a quantifiable element that indicates if it has or hasn't been achieved. Can you say, "Yes, I did this" or "No, I didn't"? If it is too ambiguous or if it's just "being the best" or "dominating the region" or "taking over the state," let's take it a step further. Who are your competitors and how many people would you serve in order to beat them? Are you competing in number of locations? Revenue size? Number of employees? *Quantify.*

DOES IT ALIGN WITH YOUR LEGACY?

The beautiful thing about owning a business is you get to decide where you're going; nobody else gets to choose this for you. And right now, if you don't have a Vision statement, you might be operating without this and you're just doing what you're doing. But think about where you want to be when you check in with yourself in ten years and ask, "Is this something that fulfills the legacy that I want to create for myself, for my team, for my family, for my community, for my customers, like, is this enough? Is this something that I can look back at and say, 'Damn, I'm proud. I really put everything into this, and I'm so grateful that I created this thing." And if it's not that, then let's rework it. Let's figure out what it is that you want to be creating because ten years is a *long* freakin' time. And if you're going to spend the next ten years putting all of this hard work into developing a team and organizing your financials and creating marketing strategies and getting kicked in the teeth when customers tell you no—you should at least get to where you want to actually go! But if that isn't clear now, all the hard work that you're distracting yourself with right now isn't going to fix that. Your legacy is not really being fulfilled or upheld by what you've chosen to put your stake in the ground for.

IS IT ONE SENTENCE?

We do not need two sentences. Or a paragraph. Or a dissertation. This should be one sentence.

IS IT EASY TO MEMORIZE?

You know the drill on this criterion from the Mission statement. If you are the only person who can memorize your Vision because it is a long-ass sentence, you've got a problem. Just shorten it. Remember what we talked about in the last chapter. Keep it tight and sweet, easy to memorize. The worst is if it's so difficult to memorize that *you* don't even memorize it. The idea is you can just rattle this Vision statement off at any moment of the day in order to create…what is that word again? What is that little C word? Confidence. Rattle that thing off. If it's not easily memorized, it's not going to create confidence in the people that you're communicating with. If you have to go look up your Vision statement, how can you expect that everyone else understands where the business is going if the leader can't?

IS IT ACTIVE VERBIAGE?

The last criterion and probably the least sexy of all the criteria is active verbiage. When you are creating your Vision statement, you do not want to say: "We have helped one million patients over the next blah, blah, blah."

There's a great exercise I do every day that comes from Grant Cardone: I write out my goals as if they've already happened. I love doing this as a way to believe that they can and already have happened. It's great, and I highly encourage you to write your *personal* goals like this too. But your team will think you're freakin' nuts if you say "We have created fifty thousand homes across America" as your Vision statement when you have only actually done five. The way that you share these statements and construct them really does matter. You will be using them on job posts, and the last thing you want to do is mislead people into thinking the business is at a future state instead of the current state. The people you need to find have to have clarity on *where* the business is going but skills relevant to where it is *today.* Active verbiage while speaking in the state of what the future looks like will do this.

AT CARDONE VENTURES

We've been clear about our Vision since we hired our first employee. That's not to say that we haven't made tweaks along the way, but we've utilized our Vision in attracting every team member who currently works at Cardone Ventures. One of the things I'm most proud of is the quality talent we have onboard. If you've ever been to a Cardone Ventures event, you know what I'm talking about. We have a group of people who are energized, passionate, and motivated to achieve their goals. At the events we host, one of the first questions from the audience is "How do I motivate my team?" and it always comes down to a lack of alignment between the owner and the team. This gap is created on the front end—you never told your candidates and new hires during onboarding where you are going. Then you get frustrated that they aren't helping you get there. At Cardone Ventures, the statements below are shared during the first interview with a candidate and are plastered all over our careers page because we're being upfront about who we are and want to attract our brand of crazy.

Our Vision statements are as follows:

Brand: Create 1 Million 10X Businesses

Revenue: $10 Billion

People: Create opportunities for 50,000 10X Employees

CLIENT SUCCESS

"The hardest part for us was always people. We didn't know how to find or attract, and we didn't know how to engage or how to show them where we're going and get them excited about making a difference. Before, we were on one page, and the staff was on another page.

Since establishing our Vision, we've been meeting with our team members and saying, 'Here's our Vision—from here, this is where we're going, and you have the opportunity to help us with that.' Our team members are excited, and it's rewarding to see them light up. We'd never even thought that we could do that."

—JANICE DOAN, A+ FAMILY DENTISTRY

EMPLOYEE **ALIGNMENT**

- ☑ MISSION
- ☑ VISION
- ☑ **CORE VALUES**
- ☐ WHERE TO USE THEM
- ☐ JOB POST
- ☐ INTERVIEW PROCESS

CHAPTER 4

CORE VALUES

CORE VALUES DEFINE YOUR CULTURE

Talking about your organization's culture became buzzworthy a decade ago. Every speaker and author I stumbled across had their own take on how to create a company culture. The widespread popularization of ping-pong tables, sleep pods, happy hours, and offsite team bonding opportunities came out of this culture craze as we all watched large tech companies like Google and Facebook incorporate these seemingly fun and work-enhancing features into their office environments. The challenge with these methods is they don't truly build culture.

Let's call them perks. To build a truly high-performing culture, you have to have clear boundaries that you use as the foundation of what behavior you want and what won't be tolerated. Core Values define these boundaries, and how you *implement* them will define your culture. You use them in the hiring process. You use them in the reward process, the retention process of your team members. And you also use them as the reason why somebody is not a fit for your organization.

I think Core Values can sometimes be challenging for people because when you're thinking about Core Values, it becomes this nebulous idea instead of a practical tool. I struggled with this for months when I first started the process of crafting company Core Values for a dental management company in 2015. Somebody first told me to write down my Core Values, and that began the belaboring process of an existential journey of questions that spiraled into asking "Who am I?" and "Why am I here?" I spent hours in this mental headspace of determining that I value life and I value relationships. Were those my Core Values? No. But without a framework, it spiraled into this really long list of ideas and tenets to live by. If you're stuck here, you're not alone, and I want to help you.

Remember: you are building a culture and using Core Values as a filtering mechanism to decide who fits and who doesn't. You're saying, "Okay, if I was to set a list of ways that I operate and that I want my team to operate, this is what that would look like, and this is how I'm going to hold my team accountable to these things."

One way to get the Core Values juices going is the following exercise:

Identify somebody in your past that you loved working with. The person you would unquestionably pick to be on any team you're a part of. What are the characteristics of that team member? Did they show up on time? Did they complete projects before they were due? Did they go above and beyond? Write down ten to fifteen characteristics of that team member.

Now, identify a past colleague that you couldn't stand working with. What characteristics didn't you like? Did you always have to follow up with them to get the work done? Did they take credit for others' work? Were they moody and negative in meetings?

Writing down those characteristics can help identify the Core Values you hold. These two lists should give you an excellent starting point for defining your five to eight Core Values. Now it's time to run them through the framework: do you have the ability to hire, reward, and fire using them?

CRITERIA
CAN YOU HIRE?

Think about the expectations you want to share with a potential new hire for your organization. In Chapter 7, I'll detail the exact questions I use in the interview process, but it's important to understand how you can use your Core Values to repel the wrong candidates and attract the right ones. You don't want just anyone to join your team; you want the best. Your Core Values should instantly communicate this with candidates. This is why I would never include a Core Value such as "fun" or "family first." It's not that fun or family is bad. But that's not what I'm going to lead with if what I'm actually looking for is someone who is fully committed and willing to do whatever it takes to be successful. Your Core Values, mixed with your Mission and Vision statements, should be used to weed out the candidates who simply don't align with the way you work, the effort you put in, and the expectations you have for everyone in your environment.

CAN YOU REWARD?

I'm going to dive deep into the reward process in Chapter 14, but it's important to note here that the Core Values should be used as a way to reward behavior through promotions and recognition.

CAN YOU FIRE?

I do want to talk about firing people. Who loves firing people? Not me. It's not fun. I've fired hundreds of team members over the past decade, and I've never enjoyed it. I recently heard someone say, "You only enjoy good things *after* you do them but rarely look forward to doing them ahead of time. Conversely, you always look forward to doing things that aren't great for you but regret it afterward." Think of exercise or eating healthy. I don't know about you, but I have *never* looked forward to a workout or eating my veggies. Not once. But afterward, I am so glad I did. The same goes with eating junk food and watching TV all day. I look forward to it and enjoy it while it's happening but don't feel great about the decision immediately after.

Firing team members is oftentimes the healthy thing to do, but it's not something you look forward to. Candidates can look so good on paper, and in the interview they say they will do anything it takes. They can check all the boxes initially, but then they start to show up late and become a bad representation of you to your clients and, more importantly, your team. You have to be able to demonstrate to your team that boundaries exist with your environment and that you have a system in place for why someone is no longer a fit. My favorite Core Value and most utilized in the firing process is results. If a team member continues to miss the mark of the role and isn't willing to gain the skills to be effective at it, the "results" Core Value is how I'm going to exit them without making the whole conversation emotional. There's no need for emotion in business. As a leader, the only reason you should inject emotion into your business is when you're celebrating results. That's where excitement comes in: when you're winning, when you're achieving, when you're hitting targets. But any drama and negativity should be thwarted by your Core Value of results.

I was speaking at a conference eighteen months ago, and after going through the Core Values explanation, I opened it up for Q&A. A woman stood up and said that our culture has a lot of demands, but where do we listen? She thought she stumped me; you know those people? Well, stumped I was not! My response was as follows: the purpose of Core Values is not to describe one-off characteristics of your environment. Do we listen to our team? Of course! But it's not a requirement that we're going to use to evaluate if someone is *successful* or not. Listening is good in certain circumstances, but we're not here to make everybody feel good and listen in a way that we're opening our culture up to being vulnerable because of our Core Values. Where I see companies go really wrong with Core Values is exemplified by a client of ours when they established a Core Value of empathy. They use their Core Values in the performance review process for their team members. Because they defined their culture as empathetic, when a team member was not doing the things she was responsible for and her manager came down on her for that, the employee then accused the company of not living up to their Core Values and not being empathetic. Well, no, no, no, no, no. We're not opening ourselves up to have our standards criticized. Leaders should be evaluated on their ability to make decisions and create results (which is one of our Core Values).

AT CARDONE VENTURES

At Cardone Ventures, our values are inescapable. No, seriously, you can't miss them. When you walk into Cardone Ventures headquarters, the very first thing you're bound to see are our six Core Values displayed on the wall. It's because we're proud of what we stand for and who we work with. But there's something even deeper and more intentional at play here.

We make our Core Values as prominent and as visible as we do because we want everyone to see them, to absorb them, and to think about them, because if you're a part of the Cardone Ventures team we want you to live them through your work. Their placement acts as a daily reminder about who we are and what we're trying to accomplish together. These Core Values are on every single job posting. You cannot apply for a position at Cardone Ventures without reading our Core Values. But if *somehow* you manage to have not read them on the post, you can't have the opportunity to join our team without making a presentation about how you align with our Core Values, as it's the third step of our interview process. Even after a candidate goes through all the screenings and we have a skills and aptitude test, the final step is to give a five-minute presentation to our executive team on experiences from your life and how they relate to our Core Values. We've made it impossible for team members to show up on their first day without having complete and entire clarity about who we are and what we're about.

Let's look at Cardone Venture's six Core Values and how they apply to our entire business:

INSPIRATIONAL

We look at how we conduct business in a very specific way. Everything that we do is bigger than we are. What do I mean by this? Well, we don't show up to work every day just for ourselves. We show up to accomplish the things that will make our team more impactful and our clients' businesses stronger, and to chase our potential so that we can achieve our personal, professional, and financial goals. Having an inspirational mindset helps make that possible.

DISCIPLINED

We do the things we say we're going to do, without exception. This dedication to discipline starts at the individual level. But we don't just think or talk about discipline; we pursue it through our actions. At Cardone Ventures, we train every single day in order to continue learning and growing to reach and then further stretch our potential. There's really no getting around it. That's how we make ourselves better. That's how we make our clients better.

ACCOUNTABLE

Accountability is central to success. We're in the business of holding ourselves and our clients highly accountable to their goals—because that's how they're achieved. True growth doesn't happen by accident. We believe that extreme accountability yields extraordinary results. And we have the track record to back that belief up.

TRANSPARENT

We're an organization that has big goals, and we move quickly. Breakdowns in communication can result in a failure to achieve those goals, so to prevent that from happening our team has transparency—across our departments, our clients, and our organization—so that we can prioritize the work we do in order to get closer to achieving our goals.

ALIGNED

We only hire growth-oriented people. Cardone Ventures can't grow if our team members aren't serious about their own personal, professional, and financial growth. When we're all in alignment about goals, opportunities, and areas of improvement, we can all win. Our teams, our clients, our entire organization is poised to win when we approach our business with an aligned mindset.

RESULTS-ORIENTED

At the end of the day, we're a business. Our clients hire us to 10X their businesses, so every product we create and every service offering we provide is designed to do one thing: deliver results. Being results-oriented as a Core Value focuses our thinking and helps us make good decisions when we're in the development stage of anything that we produce.

CORE VALUES ARE INTERCONNECTED

Did you notice anything special about the way in which our Core Values are ordered? Because that is intentional too. When you're developing your own Core Values, you need to make them clear and easy to remember, and you also need to think about their structure and flow. Our Core Values support each other. Each one leads into the next. Even their definitions are interconnected. No value lives on its own.

Additional good examples of Core Values include:

- Excellence
- Extraordinary
- Impact

- Intentional
- Commitment
- Production
- Determination
- Responsibility
- Ownership

CLIENT SUCCESS

"We had had a culture that was just kind of getting by.

I signed up for the People Essentials Workshop because it was our biggest pain point. Without a doubt it was a defining moment in our company. It has really acted as a fundamental process for everything going forward. For me, the greatest takeaway was really establishing clarity through the Mission, the Vision, and then the Core Values. The Core Values—I can't even tell you—it's everything.

We had one top performer, as most offices have, that felt she was an all-star. She was very defiant to rules, and 90 percent of our attention was put on to her. You think you need this person, you think you're living and dying by this person, you think the business would crack without her. But she was keeping things back. We rolled out Core Values and could see tremendous resistance occurring.

She was challenged. I coached her that change can be difficult but it's going to make her and the team better. I was going to have one more alignment discussion with her, but she self-selected out and quit.

I knew I allowed this culture to function and lead, so that was my fault, but by staying true to the process, staying true to the Core Values, it has only made the team stronger. When that person self-selected out, it was a night-and-day difference.

My one word for the Core Values is hope. It gave me hope again to dream big. You end up operating by default and in a default culture, which was not intentional in any way. But this has literally provided all the help for me to dream big again. We will stick to the process and Core Values. We will not deviate."

—DAVID WHITE, DDS

EMPLOYEE **ALIGNMENT**

- ☑ MISSION
- ☑ VISION
- ☑ CORE VALUES
- ☑ **WHERE TO USE THEM**
- ☐ JOB POST
- ☐ INTERVIEW PROCESS

66*99*

CHAPTER 5

WHERE TO USE YOUR MISSION, VISION, AND VALUES

Once you've created your Mission, Vision, and Core Values, put them everywhere. Seriously. Make it a part of your business's letterhead. Put it in your email signatures. Plaster it everywhere you possibly can so that you, your team, and prospective candidates (aka everyone who comes in contact with you) know exactly what it is that you're about. Places include the following:

- Job posts
- Interview process
- Performance review conversations
- All-team meetings
- Email signatures
- Your website
- Employee handbook

- Onboarding checklist
- Office walls
- Letterhead

CLIENT SUCCESS

"Natalie delivers true magic where the roadmap and instruction manual was delivered with expertise and transparency. She brought to life the true brilliance behind the Cardone Venture's orchestration of the supporting systems, layering of principles, concepts, and the applications that you need to help establish your company's Mission, Vision, Core Values, and most importantly, how to seamlessly enhance your most valuable asset...your people and their development and alignment to your company's direction.

I am getting it more 'right' now than ever because of her unlocking something that truly has made a huge difference in me, personally, to bring to benefit my team and ultimately a company that is winning. I could, in fact, go on illustrating the depth of knowledge that Natalie has to share, but I highly recommend you listen to her directly and make it your own: for you, your company, and your team of people will be better for it!"

—BLAYNE LIPAROTO, ADVANTAGE PHYSICAL THERAPY

EMPLOYEE **ALIGNMENT**

- ☑ MISSION
- ☑ VISION
- ☑ CORE VALUES
- ☑ WHERE TO USE THEM
- ☑ **JOB POST**
- ☐ INTERVIEW PROCESS

66/99

CHAPTER 6

JOB POST

You probably *think* you know what you want when it comes to your ideal team members, but have you ever taken the time to actually document it? Let's stop thinking and start *doing* so you can finally surround yourself with the people who can help you achieve your recently defined Mission and Vision.

When it comes to hiring good employees, you have to be perfectly clear—with yourself and in your job post—about what it is that you want. You need to write down *the exact* things that you're looking for. If you don't take the time to do this, well, you're not gonna get what you want. Period.

What do I do to clarify what I want, set expectations, and create a framework for my ideal candidate? No matter what the role is, I consult the following job post checklist. No fluff. No job technicalities. Just the essentials. You certainly can tailor this content to reflect your own business's image, but with each addition I would challenge you to reflect and ask yourself, "Why? Why is it important to add this?"

I've hired hundreds of incredible team members and helped business owners all over the nation do the same. The checklist is proven to be effective—partially out of trial and error, and partially out of using data that is already out there.

According to Peter Economy's "11 Interesting Hiring Statistics You Should Know" for *Inc.*, the five most important considerations candidates look at when considering job offers (your goal is to find someone you want to make an offer to, right?) are, as follows:

1. Salary and compensation
2. Career growth opportunities
3. Work-life balance
4. Location and commute
5. Company culture and values

If you're not including details that pertain to the above, you're not including information that your candidates care most about. And if we're going to create an effective job post, we need to think about mindset—yours *and* that of your ideal candidate. Listen, when you're writing a job post, you shouldn't be doing it from the perspective of a hiring manager or a human resources representative; you need to be a marketer! In this instance, your candidates are your potential customers. What are the features, advantages, and benefits of a career in your organization?

Look at competitor job postings. Look at similar job postings across comparable industries. How can you differentiate your organization from the pack to get the best possible talent vying for your attention? How are you speaking to career growth opportunities? You're reading this because we share an alignment in growing our businesses through growing our people, so clearly spell out *how* you do that in your job posting.

CRITERIA

So, for the purposes of this checklist exercise, let's create a post based on our need to hire a chief financial officer. This example is actually the exact post we used to hire our CFO at Cardone Ventures. The candidate applied within three days of posting, and we hired him within two weeks (more to come on crafting the interview process in the next chapter). Here are the exact things you need to include.

POSITION SUMMARY

Three to five sentences outlining the purpose of this role. *This* role creates *this* ideal outcome. Don't know this information? Then I'd question why you're hiring for the role in the first place. You're adding staff to your company because they're going to create a specific, critical, quantifiable value or set of quantifiable values. Set those expectations here.

You should also be thinking of this summary as sales copy. The point of the post is to attract the talent you want in order to fill the role. If it's dull and too corporate, the right person will be less inclined to hit apply. The unique elements of the role should be described here in a way that will interest the potential candidate. Who they're reporting to, strategic elements of their role, all the fun (but not too fun that it's misleading) components should be included in this section.

CFO Example

The Chief Financial Officer (CFO) is responsible for reviewing potential strategic business partnerships for operational and financial opportunities and risks. As a true business partner to the Chief Executive Officer (CEO), the CFO is responsible for the overall organizational performance in regard to both the annual budget and the brand's long-term strategy. The CFO will develop tools and systems to provide critical financial and operational information to the CEO and make actionable recommendations on both strategy and operations. The CFO will ensure that long-term budgetary planning and costs management are in alignment with the brand's strategic plan, especially as the organization considers sponsorships, potential acquisitions, and collaborations with external organizations.

The position is also responsible for identifying, determining, and supporting key relationships by seeking to understand the client's needs for long-term growth. Ultimately, a successful CFO will provide excellent business insights and guidance and will collaborate with our CEO and executive team to create successful long-term business partnerships.

ABOUT US

Now, this is more strategic than you might think. You don't include a summary about your organization just to promote yourselves. You include a company summary to equip the candidate with what they need to know in order to get a foundational understanding of why you exist, where you are going, and how the culture is defined. Sound familiar? *This* is where you include your Mission, Vision, and Values into your hiring process to filter out the candidates that you don't want while exciting the ones that you do. Seriously. There's intentionality behind it. You want people who have the same level of ambition, problem-solving skills, and thirst for growth that you do, and this is how it's done.

This portion of the job post should get them researching and absorbing everything they possibly can about the organization so that when you ask them, "What do you know about our company?" they can express their enthusiasm, curiosity, and self-motivation through their answer. This is the first question I ask on any interview because it separates the serious from the average. I like to think of this as follows: If I was going to interview somewhere, what amount of research would I do? Would I wing it? Absolutely not. Now, I don't expect that a candidate will spend hours poring through our website and social pages, although some do, but I do expect them to read the post they applied for. I am giving them the answers to the homework assignment in plain sight. If they didn't care to read the "About Us" portion, they're not the right fit.

Cardone Ventures Example

Our Mission is to help business owners achieve their personal, professional, and financial goals through the growth of their businesses. We work in dozens of verticals and provide strategic business guidance through courses, live events, partnerships, and investments. Our Core Values are the backbone of our business and guide our hiring process: we are inspirational, disciplined, accountable, transparent, aligned, and results-oriented. This company operates nationally and is growing by the day.

OBJECTIVES

The objectives outlined in a job posting should give focus to the specific work of a specific role. Each one of these objectives should be built upon the team member achieving certain outcomes based on the departmental goals, and desired team and individual outcomes. This means you not only need to be intentional about the objectives you're including in the job posting, but also in terms of priority. Again, it's filtering. If the candidate can't fulfill the first objective, they certainly aren't going to be able to achieve those that come afterward.

When I review my client's posts, I chuckle when they list "making coffee" and "greeting the clients" above "twenty-five outbound phone calls per day." Keep the main thing the main thing. As a side note, I would never list "making coffee" or "vacuuming" on a job post. You should be creating a high-level bucket that captures small things the team member would be doing such as "Prepare the office for a remarkable client experience." Ten to fifteen *prioritized* objectives should be your target.

CFO Example

- Develop the financial foundation of the organization by providing financial projections, accounting oversight, and growth plans.
- Develop and establish financial, organizational strategies by using financial and accounting information, analysis, and recommendations to inform strategic thinking and direction and by establishing functional objectives in line with organizational objectives.
- Develop and report financial strategies by forecasting capital, facilities, and staff requirements; identifying monetary resources; and developing action plans. This is for Cardone Ventures as well as partners.
- Monitor financial performance by measuring and analyzing results, initiating corrective actions, and minimizing the impact of variances.
- Maximize the return on invested funds by identifying investment opportunities and maintaining relationships with the investment partners.

- Accomplish the financial and organizational Mission by completing related tasks as needed.
- Plan, implement, and manage investment strategies, and determine financial and operating metrics for Cardone Ventures and investment partnerships.
- Adhere to the law and the company's policies.
- Coordinate audits and proper filing of taxes.
- Update job knowledge by remaining aware of new regulations, participating in educational opportunities, reading professional publications, maintaining personal networks, and participating in professional organizations.
- Represent the company to financial partners, including financial institutions, investors, foundation executives, auditors, public officials, etc.
- Manage the company's audit (if applicable) and tax preparation by coordinating with external professionals as necessary.

COMPETENCIES

The difference between objectives and competencies? Objectives are things an employee is expected to accomplish, whereas competencies are the skills they bring with them to the organization in order to achieve their objectives. An example would be negotiating skills if the role you're hiring for requires negotiation in order to achieve the objectives. A tip: if you struggle coming up with competencies you're looking for, evaluate some of the negative experiences you've had with team members in the same role. If they were too tactical and couldn't come up with strategy, list "able to formulate and present strategy" as a competency. The things they were lacking to get the job done go in the competencies list, and, of course, we prioritize those, too.

CFO Example

- Solid generally accepted accounting principles (GAAP) and financial reporting, technical skills
- All stages of acquisition experience
- Working knowledge of taxation and corporate structures
- Financial planning and strategy
- Managing profitability
- Cash planning
- Strategic planning and vision
- Proficiency with word processing and spreadsheets
- Quality management
- Promotion of process improvement
- Forecasting
- Budget development
- Corporate finance
- Acquisition support
- Transaction, partnership, taxation structures

EDUCATION AND EXPERIENCE

The education and experience section is pretty straightforward and, depending on the type of role you're hiring for, is only as important as you think it needs to be. In most roles, I don't place too much emphasis on education. I'm looking for intelligent, driven people, but that doesn't necessarily mean that everyone has to have an MBA. In some instances, a person with a high school diploma will be more valuable than someone who has finished several degrees. If you're willing to do the hard work, get the results we need, and keep striving, that's what matters most to us.

It depends on the person, but as a rule of thumb, I'm more interested in assessing "will" than "skill." Skills can be trained and developed. Willingness to learn and grow can't be taught.

CFO Example

- Certified public accountant (CPA) certification and Big Four firm experience a plus
- Prior CFO in a public company, midsize to large
- Minimum ten years' experience in accounting and financial management practices
- Required experience: private equity, raising capital debt equity, mergers and acquisitions, multi-location expansion and operations, and consolidations/roll ups

PHYSICAL REQUIREMENTS

This is even more straightforward than the education and experience piece. Is the person in this role going to be sitting at their desk all day long? Will they be on their feet? What are their travel requirements? What are the physical requirements needed to do the job that's being advertised?

CFO Example

- Prolonged periods sitting at a desk and working on a computer
- This position will require travel: up to 50 percent

COMMITMENT TO DIVERSITY

I can't overstate the importance of this section. You need to be explicit that your organization is committed to diversity *while actually being committed to diversity.* Having a team of people from all different types of backgrounds and viewpoints will help your organization thrive, be stronger, serve a broader base of clients, and be more innovative. It's just that simple.

Cardone Ventures Example

As an equal opportunity employer committed to meeting the needs of a multigenerational and multicultural workforce, Cardone Ventures recognizes that a diverse staff, reflective of our community, is an integral and welcome part of a successful and ethical business. We hire local talent at all levels regardless of race, color, religion, age, national origin, gender, gender identity, sexual orientation, or disability, and actively foster inclusion in all forms both within our company and across interactions with clients, candidates, and partners.

CALL TO ACTION

Of course, any job post—whether you're using a recruiting platform or your own internal HR team—needs a strong call to action for candidates who are interested in being a part of your organization. But what we like to do is include small details in our job posts that inspire the real go-getters out there to differentiate themselves from the rest of the applicants, to create an opportunity to stand out. Similarly, look for those applicants that are doing something beyond what's normal, standard practice for applying for a job. Those people that are going against the grain—whether they're sending video with their resumes, figuring out how to reach out directly to hiring managers and organizational leadership, or flexing their worth in some other unusual way—are showing you one of their competencies. Pay attention to these special people.

I always add the following statement to every job post: "If this position caught your eye, send us your resume! For best consideration, include the job title and source where you found this position in the subject line of your email to careers@

yourcompanyname.com. Already a candidate? Please connect directly with your recruiter to discuss this opportunity."

This gives an opportunity for the high performers to self-identify. Pro tip: track the source of every hire. Just like client leads, your team leads are important in order for you to get more of the good and less of the bad.

EMPLOYEE **ALIGNMENT**

☑ MISSION

☑ VISION

☑ CORE VALUES

☑ WHERE TO USE THEM

☑ JOB POST

☑ **INTERVIEW PROCESS**

CHAPTER 7

INTERVIEW PROCESS

If you've ever regretted making certain hires for your organization, maybe you need a new approach. I hate to break it to you, but sometimes it's not them, it's *you*. At the end of the day, if you're repeatedly hiring the wrong people for your organization, then you bear responsibility for creating these outcomes. Some people interview really well, and then once they've landed the job and the actual work begins, they turn out to not be a great fit. Others—those diamonds in the rough—can get lost in the interview process because they're not being asked the right questions.

You need a better way to find better candidates to create better outcomes. I've hired hundreds of team members and developed a process to make interviewing more effective so that I can spend less time wondering if someone is "right" and more time scaling the business.

Your time is valuable. So is the time of the people who are

looking for the next phase of their careers. In respect of this, I've created a three-step process for interviewing that is oriented around Cultural-, Operational-, and Core Values-based questions and presentation sections.

This not only establishes the essential consistency that is needed for interviewing and hiring the right people for the organization, but it also ensures that we're aligned in the areas that matter most to both parties. And I do mean *both* parties. If our interviewees can't be bothered with Cultural, Operational, and Core Value alignment, it's glaringly obvious that we're wasting one another's time.

I don't want to waste my time. I want to grow this business. I want team members dedicated to the Mission, just like you want team members dedicated to your business's Mission.

So let's dive into this process.

THE CULTURAL INTERVIEW

This part of the interview process is where I'm seeking the answer to the question, "Do they have the behavioral attributes necessary to be culturally aligned?"

Some of you might be thinking, "Hey, I have great instincts when it comes to interviewing. I know right away whether someone is culturally aligned with our organization." And, hey, that *might* be true, but that is a rare skill, and your gut feelings aren't something that can be duplicated when you're big enough to have a recruiter (if not multiple recruiters) to keep up with the growth of your business. Besides, do you really want to be handling all of your business's interviews forever?

This is the perfect opportunity early on in the interview process to establish if the candidate is a good cultural match. These are my essential questions I ask every candidate:

QUESTION 1: WHAT RESEARCH DID YOU DO ABOUT US?

They should have done the minimum amount of research on what they can find only, but if you're a startup or don't have a big online presence, your candidate could potentially have an out…but wait! No they don't. Because you told them what they needed to know on the post they responded to! Because you are a rock star, I know that you have already utilized the structure for a kick-ass job post from Chapter 6. Remember the "About Us" section? This section provides the answer that the candidate should be able to provide. If they tell you that they don't know much about the company or couldn't find you online, say sayonara. Preparation is an essential. I would never trust someone who didn't prep for an interview (something that is important to *them*) with a client presentation or interaction (which is important to *me*).

QUESTION 2: WALK ME THROUGH YOUR PAST THREE POSITIONS AND WHAT RESULTS YOU WERE RESPONSIBLE FOR IN EACH ROLE.

With this question, I'm looking for the candidate's ability to recognize the valuable contribution they made in previous roles. They should be able to share the results the previous role drove and how they were a part of that equation. This question is open-ended enough for the candidate to take a variety of directions, and I want to see if they can stay on topic or if they're going to get on a four-minute tangent about how terrible their last boss treated team members.

QUESTION 3: WHAT PROFESSIONAL GOALS WOULD YOU LIKE TO ACCOMPLISH OVER THE NEXT FIVE YEARS?

We're going to get into how critical goal setting is in Chapter 10. This interview question is the starting point for assessing if the candidate has goals or if they're just looking for a job. I only hire growth-oriented people because there is no average in my work environment. Team members need to be able to see how working with me is the vehicle for them to achieve their goals. I once had an HR candidate share with me that she didn't have any goals because she doesn't believe that the goal-setting process works. This was an immediate no for me. If you don't believe in goals, how are you going to help our clients achieve theirs?

Goals are what drive me and every one of our team members to get up every day and do great work. So when we encounter someone who "doesn't have goals," what it's really saying to us is that this person lacks ambition, and someone who lacks ambition in their own lives certainly isn't going to have a level of ambition that helps us and our clients win. And that, my friends, is a deal breaker.

QUESTION 4: WHAT ARE YOUR SALARY EXPECTATIONS FOR THIS ROLE?

This one is straightforward. You need to have alignment in pay expectations. Ideally the salary/hourly range is shared on the post so that you don't waste your time with people who are not a financial fit for the role.

QUESTION 5: WHAT QUESTIONS DO YOU HAVE FOR US?

I find all of these questions incredibly informative, but take note of this one. I want to work with curious people. Curious people are interested in figuring things out and in solving problems. If you're interviewing someone and they have *no* questions for you, that's a red flag. You'd be surprised how often I encounter this.

BONUS QUESTIONS

What does a good day look like for you?

Describe how you communicate and show up on difficult days.

Why should we hire you?

THE OPERATIONAL INTERVIEW

It's at this stage of the interview process that I want a clear answer to the question, "Does the candidate have the technical skillset and experience to have a high level of effectiveness?"

This is a little different in that it can't be answered in a simple Q&A format. The operational phase of this process is a technical interview where we give each candidate a case study to work through that is representative of the work that they would be doing for us.

It's their responsibility to deliver a case study presentation where they present their findings, and we ask questions about their technical abilities. An added bonus is that we also get a clear sense of their presentation and communication skills. Having technical abilities is just one thing that matters to us. Good business means great communication. People have to understand where you are coming from, and the onus is on the presenter to achieve that. Some example case studies are as follows:

- Finance: create a budget, decipher a P&L
- Marketing Manager: build or review an annual marketing budget
- Graphic Design: create a logo or advertisement in ten minutes
- Project Manager: create a communication plan for a demo project
- Account Manager: rank a template SWOT analysis from least to most important

THE CORE VALUES INTERVIEW

This final interview phase is where the candidate must demonstrate alignment with our Core Values. Like phase two, this is a presentation and Q&A format, but instead of presenting on technical abilities, they are directed to cardoneventures.com/careers, where we have our Core Values posted. Then they're given five minutes to present to us how they and their work can demonstrate alignment with the Core Values of our organization, followed by a ten-minute Q&A session.

It's pretty clear when someone is aligned and when someone is not. This process has now, countless times over, helped me find the best people to push our business forward. This interview achieves two goals.

The candidate (soon to be new hire) will have memorized your Core Values before becoming a full-time team member. This reinforces that *you* take your Core Values seriously and ensures that no team member joins your company without understanding your DNA.

Additionally, this presentation is the final check if there is true alignment between the candidate and the organization's priorities. The reality is that true high performers have a track record of being disciplined, accountable, and results-oriented. They will be able to easily draw up examples in their lives that put these qualities on display. By incorporating a Core Values interview, you're reducing the chances that you'll allow an underperformer on your team.

If you want to scale your business, you need the best people, and if you want the best people, you need to be using the best processes.

EIGHT REASONS TO SAY NO

Interviewing *can* be an exhilarating experience. You're having a great discussion with someone whose experience, tenacity, and drive can help push your organization to the next level of success. What could be more exciting? However, more often than not, the interview process can be absolutely exhausting and sometimes downright frustrating.

With the business owners I've helped, one of the biggest pain points is identifying why you should pass on a candidate. It can be difficult to know what to look for if you're newer to interviewing or haven't created your dream team, so I've created this list of intolerable behaviors that can happen during the interview so that you never allow the wrong candidate into your organization. You need to weed them out before they cause the business damage. Here's what to look for.

1. THEY'RE NOT TECHNOLOGICALLY PREPARED.

We live in the age of Zoom, Google Meet, Microsoft Teams, Skype, etc. Presumably, your candidate has had days (if not longer) to prepare their technology setup well before the interview. While technical difficulties can happen, and I'm completely sympathetic to them because they can happen to all of us, there's a big difference between a slow connection and someone who clearly hasn't bothered to learn the platform before logging on to the call. If they haven't prepared *for this*, what else are they not going to prepare for?

2. THEY'RE NOT ORGANIZED TO HAVE A DISCUSSION.

I always appreciate it when an interview candidate has notes. It shows that they've done research, hopefully have insightful questions to ask, and are able to express an understanding of what the organization is all about.

But if they aren't organized enough to have their notes accessible and are causing constant delays and breaking the rhythm of the discussion because they're digging through their notes? No thanks. These are crucial business moments. You've got to be prepared. You've got to be a nimble and active participant in the discussion. And this isn't how you do it.

3. THEY DON'T KNOW HOW TO READ THE ROOM.

I'm extremely sensitive to our clientele. This means that we provide our team members with a great deal of training before they're directly interfacing with a client. So if an interview candidate suddenly starts expressing their personal political views or delving into information that is potentially divisive and has nothing to do with the business, they are showcasing a real lack of judgment. We're here to help businesses grow. Expressing these things in an interview is entirely inappropriate and should be seen as the red flag it is.

4. THEY DON'T RESPECT THE COMPANY CULTURE.

This also goes back to the idea of doing your due diligence on an organization. More than once, I've experienced a candidate expressing some pretty strong opinions about certain business practices—like cold calling in a sales context, for example—and basically blowing the interview because they didn't realize that what they were saying was in direct opposition to our culture and how we conduct business.

Now, it's up to you as the interviewer to ask clarifying questions so that you're not making assumptions. This is true for every single one of these deal breakers. Give them the opportunity to redeem themselves, but take note of how they would or would not ingratiate themselves into the company culture and how your values do (or do not) align.

5. THEIR ONLY QUESTIONS ARE ABOUT BENEFITS AND COMPENSATION.

We're looking for driven and *curious* people. What questions do they have about the organization? What sort of information are they trying to glean from the questions they are asking? I tend to think that an interviewee's questions can be even more insightful than the answers they give to mine, so when their questions are just about compensation, benefits, and vacation time, it's pretty clear that they don't understand the opportunity for their lives to change while working with us. One of our tenets: the quality of your questions will determine the quality of your results. The best question an interviewee could ever ask in my book is: can you point me to team members inside your organization who have achieved their personal, professional, and financial growth goals through working with you?

6. THEY HAVEN'T PUT IN EFFORT TO PRESENT THEMSELVES.

This is kind of related to number one, where someone hasn't gotten themselves technologically prepared to interview. Yes, we're operating in a remote world, but an interview is still an interview. How have they prepared themselves to create a good first impression? Are they dressed professionally? Are they camera-ready in the same way they (presumably) would be if they were meeting you in person? Have they put *any* effort into the environment they're in? If not, you can assume that they're going to put the same lack of effort into the business.

7. THEY INTERRUPT YOU.

An interview is a conversation. Are they giving you the space to speak? Or are they constantly interrupting you to show you how knowledgeable they are? There's a certain social dynamic taking place during an interview. Are they picking up on your cues? Are they giving your ideas room to breathe? Or are they cutting you off and, intentionally or not, being rude? This is probably exactly how they'd be with a client, so pay careful attention.

8. THEY ADD STRESS TO THE ENVIRONMENT.

I try to make a candidate feel at ease during an interview, and I always appreciate when they do the same for me. This shows me how they'd conduct themselves with our team and our clients. Never forget that they're responsible for selling themselves to you during the interview. They should be doing everything they can to make you think, "I don't think our organization can thrive *without* this person being a part of the team!"

If there's behavior during the interview that is causing you stress, this behavior is certain to persist (if not worsen) should they become a team member. Trust your instincts. Ask clarifying questions, of course, but don't ignore the red flags.

CLIENT SUCCESS

"We've been able to streamline our hiring process based on the outline and the process that Natalie has provided for us. So we've been able to attract, hire, develop, and retain these top performers. I was the first one to go through the hiring process implemented by Natalie. That's what drew me to the company. It was the job posting outline she'd created for our company that really drew me in. It's making sure you have that job posting that's going to attract the right candidates and then following through on the process. From A to Z, we've been able to implement her hiring process, and we have attracted top performers here in the company, and we're seeing the turnaround in our culture because of that as well.

With every hire we've had, we'd been able to really determine if they'd be a good fit from that hiring process. For myself in the hiring process, I knew it was the right company to work for because they were taking the time and really looking for what they could do for me instead of what I could do for them.

We've had a lot of good feedback from the hiring process. I think it's new to a lot of people. They haven't been through quite the extensive hiring process that we do, but they understand that it's weeding out the people that don't really fit in our culture, so they understand there's a reason behind it, and they actually enjoy it. We've had a lot of good compliments regarding our hiring process.

It's so important that we stick to our hiring process and implement that, and hold each other accountable to follow through; otherwise, we're never going to achieve the levels of success that we see for the company.

Everybody tells you, this is how you should do it, but gives you no instructions to follow through on how to apply it. She gives you the full step-by-step instructions, she shows you how to apply it, and she shows you how to relate it to your industry so it works for you. I think that's where she sets the bar from everyone else. She's different because she actually follows through and helps you in your personal experience."

—STEPHANIE CIBOROSKY, STRAY VOLTAGE

EMPLOYEE **DEVELOPMENT**

☑ **ONBOARDING**

☐ DAILY ALL-
TEAM MEETINGS

☐ PPF GOALS

☐ ONE ON ONES

☐ QUARTERLY
TEAM MEETINGS

☐ EMPLOYEE
MATURITY MODEL

6699

CHAPTER 8

ONBOARDING

Congratulations! You have officially hired your first new team member who is aligned with our Mission, Vision, and Core Values! It's now on us to make sure we don't fuck this up.

Trust me, I have made countless mistakes on team members' first days. They've shown up and had no place to sit, no formal onboarding plan, no equipment. I've done just about everything you can think of that was wrong for onboarding a new employee. I've even hired team members in different time zones who waited for three hours before someone called them on their first day! Whoops.

The two critical touchpoints you need to develop to ensure a smooth onboarding are a pre-arrival checklist and an onboarding plan template. I'll dive into both of these items in this chapter. As your organization grows, both of these items will evolve. Your processes will become more complex, and your departments will evolve. When you encounter a new onboarding issue (and I promise you will), make a tweak to the existing process so it never happens again. I don't want to make the same mistake twice. Now, I can assure you that it takes time to nail down this process, especially when you're a growth-oriented organization where things are changing constantly. There will most certainly be things that go wrong, but the first ninety days with a new team member are critical. So let's set them up for success.

PRE-ARRIVAL CHECKLIST

To set your new hire up for success on their first day, you'll want to create a pre-arrival checklist because there are a number of things that need to be properly prepped to ensure your new team member has everything they need to start adding value to your business immediately. Don't just wing this. Put some energy into establishing everything that needs to happen to ensure that team member can get off to the races on their first morning. Ideally, you'll develop this checklist and be able to create a consistent onboarding experience for every new team member. I think of our team member experience similarly to our client experience. There should be a standardized method for how they're greeted, welcomed, and onboarded. When a system like this is in place, you'll have confidence to add more team members.

FINALIZE THE AGREEMENTS

A major mistake I made a few years ago was not countersigning and sending back Offer Letters to our team members. I learned this lesson the hard way as I got tangled in a dispute about pay, and the employee claimed she was never provided documentation. She *was* in fact given it, and she even signed it! But it was never signed and sent back from the company. Learn from my mistakes: make sure all offer letters, employment agreements, nondisclosures, noncompetes, and anything else you send new employees are signed, dated, countersigned, and saved in their HR folder.

ESTABLISH THE NEW EMPLOYEE'S MANAGER

Once HR/Corporate knows a new hire is joining the company, they should send an email with the job description to the department head to establish who this new team member will be reporting to and what they will be responsible for. This should also be the trigger to update the organizational chart.

SEND A WELCOME EMAIL

In this welcome email, include action items the new hire will need to address before they begin work. Send over any uncompleted paperwork or contract needs. Inform them of when they should report to the office and of any parking/security matters. These things will be essential for the new hire to plan their transportation and travel time to the office.

PREPARE THE WORKSTATION

Once you know what equipment the new hire will need and where they will be sitting, contact IT so they can begin to set up their workstation. IT should be responsible for setting up any necessary company logins and email addresses.

UPDATE THE JOB DESCRIPTION

It is crucial that managers update the job description detailing what the new hire will be doing within their role. This may have been completed already if the company has filled the role before, but double-checking all objectives, competencies, and metrics before the team member starts will help create clarity. If this is a new position, an outline of the role's objectives, competencies, and metrics should be sent to HR. This will be used to properly train the new associate while also helping keep the new associate informed on what is expected of them.

INFORM THE TEAM

Once the new hire's job description is finalized, a meeting should be scheduled with the team to go over how the new hire will fit in. The new hire's manager should emphasize who this new hire will be working with, what their responsibilities will be, and how the team structure will be impacted. This will help the new hire feel welcomed while also helping to ensure everyone is on the same page.

PREPARE THE ONBOARDING PLAN

This section should have a mixture of corporate and role-specific onboarding. I have compiled what feels like millions of onboarding plans, so let's get into the critical components that you should include in your onboarding plan template.

ONBOARDING PLAN OVERVIEW

ONBOARDING PLAN INFORMATION	
Goals	To provide the knowledge and skills necessary: 1) To gain exposure to the organization's strategy and operations. 2) To gain exposure of operational objectives through team integration & examining customer data.
Time Allocation	Dedicated time with Brooke, CMO
	Dedicated time with Mike, VP of Operations
	Dedicated time with select members of internal team for exposure training
Assessment Method	Role plays with customer-scenarios will be used as an application test for knowledge/skills transfer
	Live customer integration and call assessment to elevate skills and develop customer trust

ACCESSIBILITY		
Email	jthomas@cardoneventures.com	
Accounts	CEO	Internal and Client Collaboration Platform
	CardoneU	Daily Online Training Platform
	Hubspot	CRM
	G-Suite	Email, Calendar, Document Storage, Document Creation
	Zoom	Web Conferencing
	Asana	Project Management
	Harvest	Online Time Tracking Software
	Slack	Instant Messaging

ONLINE TRAINING		
Course	Platform	Purpose
10X360 Event	CEO	To gain clarity on the customer expereience and learnings at a 10X360 event
10X Employee	CEO	To learn how to be a 10X employee at Cardone Ventures and be familar with the programs our clients team's expereince
10X Owner	CEO	To be familar with the programs we train on with our clients
10X Scale	CEO	To be familar with the programs we train on with our clients
R3	CEO	To understand your R3, how we use R3 culturally, and be a subject matter expert to our clients
CardoneU: 3 Segments everyday	CardoneU	To learn how to sell and engage customers

READING	
Book	Author
Beyond Positive Thinking	Dr. Robert Anthony
10X Rule	Grant Cardone
Sell or Be Sold	Grant Cardone
E-Myth	Michael Gerber

RESOURCES	
Document	Link
Team Contact Information	Link here
Acronym List	Link here
How to setup your signature	Link here
Cardone U Overview	Link here

OVERVIEW
Goals

Every onboarding plan should have stated goals. Why would you put your team members—your brand spanking new, perfectly aligned team members—through a process if there wasn't a *goal* for the process? Traditional onboarding structures appear to your team member like a laundry list of unnecessary tasks for them to complete. But *your* onboarding plan has been intentionally crafted, so you need to call this out. An example of an onboarding goal is "to gain exposure to the organization's strategy and operations." Another one might be "to gain exposure to operational objectives through team integrations and examining customer data." Whatever big picture you want this team member to walk away from this onboarding experience with, communicate it in the goal section. But we don't just set goals and not measure them, do we? Of course not! The final step of onboarding should include an assessment of if those goals were achieved. Did these goals get achieved? Does this team member have the clear understanding? Did they get exposure to the pieces that they needed to be exposed to? More on that shortly.

Accounts

What accounts are your new team members going to get access to and what is the purpose of each platform? When I have been onboarded in the past, it almost felt like a maze of different platforms. I wasted weeks trying to understand which platform did what. There should be an overview that shares the link and purpose of each account the team member has access to. This creates a centralized place for them to understand the purpose of each account. Pro tip: tie out training videos for how to use each account. They might not need to access all of the accounts on their first day on the job. However, it's important that the accounts are listed in a centralized area that they can always go back to.

Resources

The most important section of the overview is the resources. The resources section should be an exhaustive list of anything a brand new team member would need to know. When I look at the most successful onboarding plans that I've ever created, the resources include a variety of important information ranging from ten to fifteen core items. For starters, the employee handbook should be included as the first item in your resources list. It gives the team members everything they need to know about being a team member at the organization.

Pro tip: add a link to your company policies inside the employee handbook. Why? So you can create a policies-centered quiz in order to ensure that the policies have been read. When employees first come on board, this might seem punitive or like too much. However, when I look at our most aligned team members, they're actually appreciative that all of this information lives in one place because they know exactly what the expectations look like. They know exactly where to find information should certain situations arise, and you're doing them a favor by enforcing that this takes place early on, as it sets up the rules of engagement.

An additional item in the resources section would be team contact information so that employees can easily access who team members are along with their phone numbers or email addresses. You'll also want to include your updated organizational chart. An organizational chart is extremely important to use when creating clarity for new team members. If you don't have one, I highly suggest that you throw one together. They're easy to put together. You could open up Microsoft PowerPoint, and it would take you fifteen minutes at the most. This provides a team member with an understanding of who reports to who, which teams work together, and how the overall business flows and functions.

I also highly recommend in the resources section that you include a guide of your products and services. Every person in your organization is now an ambassador of your brand. They should be knowledgeable about what you do and compensated for bringing new clients to you. Training your team that everyone is a salesperson creates limitless growth potential. Tie out what the sales commission structure looks like for them to be able to sell so that they can add value to your business, because they're incentivized to not just do the role that they're in, but also to be able to join forces with your sales team. When you're able to mobilize an entire team around selling your products and services, you will be amazed by how fast your business can grow. Some businesses never think to set it up this way, and they only train their sales team members on how to sell. This is one of the biggest mistakes that I see, and it can be easily rectified with training and a rollout of a products and services guide in conjunction with a sales commission payout structure. This guide should be updated whenever you release a new product or service.

ONBOARDING PLAN INTERNAL TRAINING

DEPARTMENT	TEAM MEMBER	COMPLETION
Business Model Overview	Mike EVP of Operations	Complete
Client Journey	Brooke Chief Marketing Officer	Not Started
Employee Maturity Model & PPF Goals	Mike EVP of Operations	Not Started
Internal Process Review	John Business Process Specialist	Not Started

*All internal trainings have been pre-scheduled. Notify the HR team if you need to reschedule your training.

Internal training should be very structured. There are things that brand new team members need to know about all the different functions and departments of the business. The internal training section allows onboarding team members to be grouped together to hear from your leadership team about the critical areas of the business. If your business is smaller and you're not onboarding too many team members within a short period of time, you can have these meetings in a one-off setting, but you still should be able to identify the specific areas that every team member needs to learn and who is responsible for sharing that information. You should do these meetings on a One on One basis with your new team members until you hit the twenty-five team member mark. Once you hit twenty-five, these should be group trainings. At the one hundred employee mark, you should invest in turning these trainings into online courses so they scale as your team continues to grow. Here is a breakdown of what your team should be trained on.

Company Overview

The company overview would be an overview of anything that's important to your organization. You might review your org chart, resources, the business model, when and why the business was started, and the list goes on. Anything that you as the founder want all new team members to know, you should put it in a slide deck and include those things here. Your first slide should most certainly be an overview of your Mission, Vision, and Core Values.

Client Journey

How do your clients find you? What service do they start with? What service do they go to next after that service? Why do they come back? What are success stories? When you share the client journey with your team members, they will have a higher understanding of how your business functions, which will increase their responsibility for being able to sell and to contribute to this model. Devoid of this information, they aren't going to know how to solve your problems (which are *always* getting more clients). At the end of the day, as a leader, you should make it as simple as possible for the people that you have hired and chosen to bring around you to help you solve the problems that you are going to have. This client journey presentation can be as short as thirty minutes, but that thirty minutes really should map out with a flowchart and a funnel process of the journey your ideal client goes through.

Products Overview

I would also include a presentation about your products depending on how complicated your business is. Demonstrate what your product or service looks like and its features, benefits, and advantages. Show client testimonials and successes that the people you work with have had. The product overview really is a great place to dive deeper into the product. Even though somebody is in HR or accounting and they don't actually touch the delivery side or the sales side of the business, they should still be able to get a tangible understanding of what your products are and what part of the process they contribute. This will help them increase their responsibility around selling it and bringing more awareness to your brand by utilizing your highest-valued resource: your team.

Goal Setting/Opportunities

The last presentation that I would recommend is what opportunities for career advancement look like in your organization. I am the person who is responsible for giving this presentation because I don't ever want to find myself in a position where I've hired a leadership team member who is responsible for a team but doesn't actually share the true opportunity that those team members have in this organization. Setting up the process for the team member to hear, directly from you, what

career advancement looks like is important when you're thinking about expansion and your ability to develop top talent.
This presentation is certainly a time commitment but creates
the greatest opportunity for you to truly set these new team
members up for success and their understanding about what's
possible and where this organization is going. I review two specific processes called PPFs and the EMM in this presentation;
more on those in Chapters 10 and 13.

ONBOARDING PLAN
WEEK ONE

FOCUS	COMPLETION
Reach out to the following team members to scheulde a time to meet	
Operations: Mike (30 minutes)	Completed
Finance: Veronika (30 min)	Not Started
Marketing: Brooke (60 min)	Not Started
Tasks	
Setup email on cell phone	Completed
Setup your profiles in all Accounts (profile picture, name, contant info, etc)	In Progress
Download Slack on your desktop	Not Started
Submit Call Shadow Forms to Mike for review on Friday (daily)	Not Started
Send Carol a photo to use for your email signature and business cards	Not Started
Subscribe to Events calendar	Not Started
Send Carol your bio, favorite food, hobbies, and anything you want our team to know about you:)	Not Started
Meetings	
Daily All Team Meetings (Daily)	Not Started
Shadow 4 Client Calls (Everyday)	In Progress
End of week touchbase with Supervisor (Friday)	Not Started
Online Training	
10X360 Event	Completed
10X Employee	In Progress
CardoneU	
3 Segments everyday	Not Started
Reading	
The 10X Rule – Grant Cardone	Not Started

Now that we've gone through the overview, the first four weeks of a new team member's onboarding should be detailed in a weekly breakdown. The internal meetings will happen throughout the course of the first month, but the weekly tasks should take place in the week that they are assigned. I recommend a four-week onboarding for any team member that joins your organization. There are certain roles that need more training because their roles are more technical in nature, but for the most part, every role should be able to onboard within a four-week time period. Each week is broken down into four distinct sections: meetings, tasks, online training, and reading.

Meetings

Make sure to include your new team member in all meetings they need to attend. It sounds straightforward and it is. Spend five minutes going through the calendar for the upcoming month and include them on any project launches, updates, and kickoffs they'll need to be a part of. It can take weeks, sometimes even months, to remember to add new employees to recurring meetings if you don't spend this time on the front end. Really map out who they should be meeting within their first four weeks to get the information they need.

Tasks

The task section is certainly the most transactional part of the onboarding, but there are certain things that absolutely need to be done that you don't want to forget when you're bringing a new team member on. These things might be as simple as setting up their email on their cell phone, putting all of their pictures and account information in their new platforms, downloading apps on their desktops, updating their LinkedIn profile to their new position, things of that nature. We also recommend that they complete their employee handbook quiz in the first week. Throughout the course of their four-week onboarding, they will mark the status of each of these items as either complete, in progress, or not complete.

Online Training

Any sort of online training that you require for your team should be included in the breakdown for which weeks they are currently onboarding. This could include YouTube videos, courses, sexual harassment training, and setting the expectations for any internal systems where you already have recurring trainings, such as Cardone University.

Reading

One of the most cost-effective forms of development is through reading books. For $15 per book, you can teach a team member how to approach problem solving and leadership from a different perspective. I highly recommend making reading a mandatory component of your onboarding process. This allows time for them to develop and to start thinking the same way that you think. Clearly you're reading this book right now, and you know how impactful and how important learning new ideas and concepts is. So for every week during onboarding, I recommend having a book identified that has changed you at some part of your leadership journey. That way, you can impart that knowledge to your team members. This speeds up the onboarding and development process significantly because *you* don't have to teach these things. The author has already put the work into the book, and the team member gets to be impacted by the words. This ultimately creates what you're looking for: teammates who are thinking like you and who are able to solve bigger problems.

Our required readings are:

- *Beyond Positive Thinking* by Dr. Robert Anthony
- *The 10X Rule* by Grant Cardone
- *Sell or Be Sold* by Grant Cardone
- *E-Myth* by Michael Gerber

ONBOARDING RECAP AND SURVEY

The final step is the onboarding recap meeting. This thirty-minute meeting should be used to dive in with that new employee to understand their onboarding experience and what can be improved. This meeting serves to ensure that all of the components of the onboarding process are complete and gives the team member a check-in. There is *a* lot of information and things to do during the first four weeks, and it's just as important for the team member to have a check-in as it is for you to make sure everything ran smoothly. In the beginning, you will want to be conducting these check-ins yourself, but as you grow, your dedicated HR person should be leading these conversations. Here's my recommended agenda for these meetings.

REVIEWING THE ONBOARDING PLAN

When you review the onboarding plan, it's important to note that all of the items were completed. If you're just issuing onboarding plans and not actually looking to see that they're completed, it's very likely that team members will miss certain pieces. And if they're missing pieces, why would you put them in there originally, if they're not required?

GENERAL FEEDBACK

The second piece is any general feedback that the team member has to share. This gives them space to say something positive or share an area of opportunity. Ideally, your team member feels safe to share honest feedback during this time.

PPF CONVERSATION

The third piece is to ensure that a date is established for that team member's personal, professional, and financial goal conversation. We dive deep into this process in a later chapter, but it's important to note that there should be some checks and balances here. It is the manager's responsibility to get this scheduled, but HR should be tracking this activity.

ONBOARDING QUIZ

It's important to inspect what you expect. The quiz should tie out to your goals on the overview tab of your onboarding plan.

NEW HIRE SURVEY

The final step is actually issuing a new hire survey. This is optional for the employee to complete, but we do encourage them to do it. This survey gets more specifics from them as to how their experience has been so far and what you can do differently next time by improving your process. I've found gold in these surveys and read every single one. I break down the areas of feedback into three sections: the recruitment section, the onboarding section, and the general section.

Recruitment

1. Rate your overall experience with our hiring process. (1–10)
2. What did we do well?
3. Is there anything about it that you would have changed?
4. Compare the organization to what we explained it would be like.

Onboarding

1. Rate your overall experience with our onboarding process. (1–10)
2. What did we do well?
3. Is there anything about it that you would have changed?
4. Is there something we should provide to new employees that we missed?

General

1. What do you like about the job?
2. What do you like about the organization?
3. What can the organization do to help you become more successful in your job?
4. Is there anything you would like to add?

* * *

Now that your plan is prepared, it's time to get ready for the first interaction your new team member will have as an official employee: the daily all-team meeting.

EMPLOYEE **DEVELOPMENT**

- ☑ ONBOARDING
- ☑ **DAILY ALL-**
  TEAM MEETINGS
- ☐ PPF GOALS
- ☐ ONE ON ONES
- ☐ QUARTERLY
  TEAM MEETINGS
- ☐ EMPLOYEE
  MATURITY MODEL

66/99

CHAPTER 9

DAILY ALL-TEAM MEETINGS

Daily all-team meetings are the most effective way to align your team daily on the cultural, operational, and financial status of the business. It's more than a list of to-dos—it's a means of focusing on how your business is winning and energizing the *entire team* to achieve what's possible. I'm surprised by how often I get asked to cover this topic, but upon reflection, I understand why. If you've ever had the pleasure of visiting Grant Cardone's headquarters, then you get it. Every morning, the entire staff—all 150-plus of them—gathers together. There's music blasting; there's a real palpable, positive energy that fills the space, and it is inspiring. It makes you want to tackle the day with your whole being, give it everything you've got, and then give it some more.

We took that feeling with us when we came back to the Cardone Ventures offices eighteen months ago with the goal of starting every business day in the exact same way. In my prior companies, we had all-team meetings, but they weren't daily, and they certainly weren't like this. In 2020 when our Cardone Ventures team started working remotely, it forced me to rethink our approach. I knew the feeling we wanted to create and the level of focus we needed to instill into our team members. But would the virtual nature of our meetings be a hindrance to achieving this?

Here's the thing: we didn't know, but we were committed to doing it. It wasn't going to be perfect, but we were going to get better at it by following through on that commitment. That's my first recommendation to you before we dive into the meat of this. Just commit to these daily meetings. When you commit, it's incredible how quickly the organization will prioritize getting the right reporting and structure in place. If you don't currently have structure, you shouldn't wait to implement this meeting until you do; you should implement the meeting so it *forces you to create it*. This works like magic.

PART 1: WELCOME TO WORK!

You welcome clients to meetings. You might say good morning to coworkers and exchange pleasantries, but do you really *welcome* your team to work? Most organizations do not. It's overlooked. Use this time at the start of the meeting to help people shed those nonwork-related concerns—the laundry and the dishes and partner and kid and house stuff that can distract you from doing your best work.

When you pump each other up about the work, you can achieve great results. When you can achieve great results, you can apply the fruits of your efforts (money, an improved mood or outlook, or other perks) to the non-work things. Be intentional about this time. Use it as the opportunity it is to inspire and shake out the yawns and the stress and the bullshit so we can all get excited about doing great work.

PART 2: WINS AND PRIORITIES

The next part of the daily all-team meeting is for each department to share their wins from yesterday and their priorities for the day. Focusing on wins energizes the team and is a daily reminder of what we've shown up to do: win. Structure your wins by department, and don't do this randomly. At Cardone Ventures, we lay it out in accordance with our client journey. It starts with Marketing and then moves on to Sales, then Accounting, Events, Learning and Development, Platform Review, and then our Strategic Business Unit.

I recommend you structure yours similarly based on *your* client cycle. And make sure to make this communication of wins very focused. This isn't a quarterly update. This isn't about future, visionary goals. This is, quite specifically, what each team was able to achieve *yesterday*. No more, no less. What KPIs did you improve yesterday? How many client meetings did you conduct yesterday? How much cash did you collect yesterday?

Having these daily updates can help us identify micro trends with clients and how we should structure future outreach. Can you see where I'm headed with this? This is where the day's priorities come into play. Our daily priorities come into very clear focus when we're discussing yesterday's wins and we all have a clear sense of what our departmental and company goals are.

PART 3: SHARE SOMETHING YOU'RE LEARNING

At Cardone Ventures, we have a daily learning and development platform called Cardone University. It helps us grow as individuals and as team members, promotes career development, and helps our people achieve their personal, professional, and financial goals because it teaches them how to *sell*. Everything you want in life comes down to a sale: selling yourself, your clients, your team, your spouse. This training is truly transformational, and we wanted an active way for people to showcase their experience with the material.

When I first introduced this, we only had eleven team members, so I literally put everyone's name in a hat, drew one at random, and, without exception, that person had the floor for the next few minutes to share what they learned the day before during their training. Today, we have a fancy wheel that feels like we're playing the Wheel of Fortune! This exercise reinforces that not just training but *learning* is a priority. It helps improve our team's comprehension of the material, their presentation skills, and their sales chops, and fosters thinking and discussion from the rest of the team.

After the team member shares what they learned, they role-play with a sales team member to ensure they know how to utilize the material. It can certainly be intimidating at first, especially for new team members, but it sets the tone for our culture. We are about improvement and remove our egos in the process. You should never let your team members practice on your clients; role-play is a game changer to get reps in.

If you want to turn your entire team into sales professionals and help them achieve their personal, professional, and financial goals, check out Cardone University today at cardoneuniversity. com.

PART 4: REINFORCE YOUR BUSINESS'S CORE VALUES

Our leadership is composed of published authors who have written multiple books that speak directly to the Mission, Vision, and Core Values of our organization. At random, we'll grab one of those books, open it to a page—literally any page—and read a passage from it.

The point? There's knowledge to be gleaned from every single one of those pages, and they reinforce the impact we're making on ourselves and our clients' lives by showing up and doing the work. We're here for a reason. Is every single action we're taking that day in service of helping transform our clients? If not, we've got to adjust.

Of course, not every business has published authors in its midst. I get that. Pick up a copy of *The 10X Rule* by Grant Cardone and you can implement the same learnings and end your meetings with energy!

Your daily meetings don't need to be a slog. In fact, they shouldn't be. They are a daily opportunity. Are you taking advantage of them?

CLIENT SUCCESS

"Our team meetings are held every day at 9:30 a.m. Before learning the proper structure, the meetings consisted of me just rambling about whatever issue was bothering me or whichever agent was complaining the most. It has not been easy to break the habit, but through making it a priority and having a defined agenda, our team knows what we will be talking about and has become more focused and aligned. Our big goals are being met as we fill the holes in our boat so more time is being spent focusing on KPIs that produce income. Having the team aligned has increased our profits by 15 percent, and our agents have had their best months ever in real estate."

—PARNELL QUINN, THE SIMPLE LIFE REALTY

EMPLOYEE **DEVELOPMENT**

- ☑ ONBOARDING
- ☑ DAILY ALL-
  TEAM MEETINGS
- ☑ **PPF GOALS**
- ☐ ONE ON ONES
- ☐ QUARTERLY
  TEAM MEETINGS
- ☐ EMPLOYEE
  MATURITY MODEL

CHAPTER 10

PPF GOALS

This personal, professional, and financial goals process changed my life. During my summer internship when I was twenty years old, I reported to the VP of Administration, who took me under her wing and gave me insight into the different projects and opportunities within the organization. At the two-month mark of my employment, she asked me to start formulating my personal, professional, and financial goals for the next one, three, and five years. I remember sitting at my desk staring at a blank legal pad for hours. I had never put my goals into such concrete buckets. I had always thought of my goals as a wish list that felt far-off and idealistic. But I had an assignment and was determined to complete it so I could have my PPF conversation with her. Here is what I came up with.

Personal:

- Find supportive friends
- Eat one green thing every day

Professional:

- Be a manager and lead a team
- Travel monthly for work

Financial:

- Save $5K to put down in order to buy a nicer car (I desperately wanted to get rid of my 1993 Buick Century)
- Make $15 per hour

I felt silly writing these down. You know that feeling? You put down in writing what you really want, and it seems so unattainable compared to where you're currently at. At the time, I was in the middle of college, still financially dependent on my parents, and had no idea what I wanted to do with my economics degree. Despite feeling silly, I couldn't lie to myself. This short list was *exactly* what I wanted, and I could close my eyes and imagine being a confident businesswoman leading teams and rolling around in a new car. This seemingly silly exercise transformed my life and was the starting point for the goal-oriented, make-it-happen person I am today.

Every team member should have the same opportunity I had: a manager who cared about my goals and pushed me to figure out what I really wanted so that she could help coach me to get there. We're going to dive into how to make this PPF process a staple in your organization, but before we dive in, it's important to introduce the concept of ME versus WE roles.

ME VERSUS WE ROLES

Every role inside your organization is categorized as a ME role or a WE role, whether you've identified them or not.

ME role: responsible for work that produces an outcome.

WE role: responsible for leading team members.

ME VS WE ORG CHART

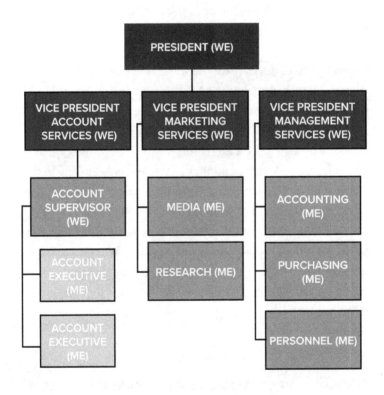

You should never have a person in a WE position unless they have been able to demonstrate that they could do the ME work. In an ideal scene, you've created an organization where the people who are leaders (WE roles) have demonstrated competency in being able to excel at the work the team they are managing is responsible for. Their competency is what gives them credibility. It is so important that your organization is structured like this because WE leaders aren't bosses or just managers—they are coaches to everybody that reports to them. And if you've put people in leadership positions that have never actually done what they're asking their team members to do, you have violated this primary leadership principle. Whether you acknowledge it or not, you are attracted to learn from people who are in more senior positions than you. Who've been able to create something that you haven't.

When you have a ME leader in a role, what you are implying from the structure is that the ME team member's goal should be to duplicate the results of the WE leader. This would make sense *only* if the WE leader has actually done what the ME leader is trying to do. The reason this is important is when it comes to the PPF conversation, the ME leader is looking to the WE leader as a coach to get them to the next level. A coach can't give guidance on something they've never done or have no knowledge about. So all WE leaders have to be able to identify goals, put a plan in place, hit milestones, and actually complete the goal. But if the people you've put in leadership positions haven't actually achieved their goals, how are they supposed to help somebody else go from setting to achieving a goal? If you *can't* do, you can't teach.

PERSONAL, PROFESSIONAL, AND FINANCIAL GOALS

The personal, professional, and financial goal structure creates buckets to organize any goal a person can have. These three categories touch everything. After having over five hundred-plus PPF conversations to date, I've yet to come across a goal that doesn't fall into one of these buckets.

- **Personal goals**: Personal goals encompass a whole wide variety of things from a personal standpoint that people can be motivated by: working out, playing the clarinet, traveling abroad, spending time with loved ones, learning a new language, becoming a great baker. They run the gamut. It will surprise you what some of your team members' personal goals are, and I can promise that you will learn something unexpected with every PPF conversation you have.
- **Professional goals**: Professional goals are focused on areas of accomplishment. This includes learning new skills, learning new ways of operating, taking on new responsibilities, being promoted, starting new projects, receiving awards or recognition for those efforts, and attracting mentors into your life.
- **Financial goals**: Financial goals are focused on things that inspire motivation. This could be your net worth, establishing passive income, having the ability to purchase gifts, paying off school loans, being able to afford family care services, target salary, paying off debt, etc.

By breaking down individual goals into these three categories, the actions required to accomplish these goals can be more focused and intentional. This helps create the overall plan and compartmentalize the goals in a structured format, which is essential because we find that most people don't plan to fail... they simply fail to plan.

WHY INCLUDE PERSONAL GOALS?

Why do you think we ask about personal goals in a work context? There's rarely pushback on the professional and financial, seeing as though both of those categories are tied to the work the team member does with you. But personal is just as important because the reality is that our team members are not robots. As nice as it would be to hire people who only want to work eighteen hours a day and who eat, breathe, and sleep our business, that's just not reality. People work to be able to fund and create an impactful personal life with the people they care about. Your team members want to buy a boat to hang out on the river during a hot summer day and be able to take their family on trips. Others are motivated by overcoming their fears by doing standup comedy once a month or running a marathon. So to the extent that you're just ignoring this whole side of your team members' lives, you're missing a big component of what's driving them. And as their coach, it's critical to know what truly drives and inspires to get the best out of them. That's your job.

Think for a moment about your own personal, professional, and financial goals. Even for the most career-driven people, when you look at their goals, the conquest is *part* of why chasing financial goals is so thrilling, but the ability to put yourself, your family, and the people you care about in a position to thrive *personally* is oftentimes the root of the true motivation. Your team is no different, which is why the personal goals come first and often take the most time to establish.

THE LEADER'S GOALS

Before you go and set the expectation that your team members need to be goal-oriented and share these goals with their manager, I need to remind you that the culture of setting and sharing goals starts at the top. As the leader of the organization, whether you thought it was your responsibility until now or not, you need to make your goals clear to the team.

To the extent that you're not sharing your goals, you're

missing one of the most transformational elements of any high-performing team. When you start talking about things that you're going after, it inspires the people in your environment. It reinforces that you're creating a high-performance team because *you're* a high performer. You should have so much confidence in where you're going because you're committed to doing the work every single day to push your goals forward.

Before we move on to the process for your team's goals, I want you to write down your goals. This should take you thirty minutes. Once you've written them out, I want you to identify which goals you're going to start sharing with your team. By no means do you need to share everything with them, but choose the goals that you are willing to share and start publicly going after them. When I say "share," I don't mean schedule a meeting with your entire team to walk through your goals. I have a feeling that wouldn't go over well. What I mean is start finding ways to publicly share which goals you're currently going after. If you want to complete a half marathon, start sharing on social media your training schedule and a countdown to race day. If one of your goals is to spend more time with your significant other, share that date night is a priority and document it. You should always be promoting these areas of growth that you're targeting. Grant Cardone shares his goals by wearing a shirt that says, "Billionaire in the Making." This is the perfect example of sharing a current goal he's going after. My fiancé and I are getting married in a few months, so I've started to go live on Instagram during my workouts to take people along on the journey. While I've been writing this book, I've been sharing updates on how many words I've written and how many I have left to hit my target. This doesn't just promote my goals to our team; it also promotes them to clients, prospective clients, competitors, and candidates. There should be no confusion for anyone that your culture is goals-oriented, and that starts with you.

The biggest goal that you should be promoting all the time is your Vision. Your Vision statement should be your ultimate professional goal. There shouldn't be a day that goes by where you don't talk about your Vision to someone.

ARE YOU SURE?

You don't *have* to implement this process. There are many businesses that don't. Before you jump feet first into this PPF process, these are the three requirements you need to be aware of:

DEEPLY CARE

You have to deeply care about your team members. If you have low regard for them and choose to believe that your success isn't integrally tied to their success, there's no need to roll this process out. This isn't just a tool to implement to pretend like you care or to try to fabricate a high-performing culture. Your team will smell the insincerity a mile away. This only works when the leader is truly bought into the idea that they are in the people business and that their team's success matters.

COMMIT

Once you roll out this process, you need to make a commitment to it because you cannot just have a PPF conversation with the people you like and not have it with others. Everyone should have the same opportunities inside your organization, and rolling it out to everyone removes bias, playing favorites, and nepotism.

I know you're tired of having me remind you how important the org chart is, but it has to be said: with a process like this, your org chart should guide who is having the conversations, and tying out a tracker to it will ensure that everyone used the same process. It might seem unnecessary if your whole team reports to you, but it's the right way to set it up so that it's organized as you grow and add more team members.

FOLLOW THROUGH

Early in my career, one of the worst mistakes I made in the PPF process was having goal conversations with people and then never talking about them again. I failed in my role as a coach. You have to remember that goals are sensitive to most people because it's an acknowledgment of something they want but don't know how to get or have tried and failed in the past. A goal wouldn't be a goal if it was easy or if you had already done it. So there's already this hesitation your team members will have about sharing them. Once they do, you need to be responsible for following through. You don't get to sit back and watch them fail because if they're quitting on *their* goals, what makes you think they're going to continue to fight for *yours*?

THE PROCESS

It's not an event. It's not just a one-time conversation. It is a process. Setting individual goals provides your team members the opportunity to establish a long-term vision and create short-term motivation. Our process is:

- Introduce:
  - Website
  - Careers page

- ◦ Job description
- ◦ Interview process
- • Onboard:
  - ◦ Overview presentation
  - ◦ Conversation at sixty days
- • Perpetuate:
  - ◦ Daily clarity through an incentive plan
  - ◦ One on One
  - ◦ Quarterly team meeting celebrations

Because this process is at the core of our business, we introduce the PPF conversation at every candidate touchpoint: It's shared in the job descriptions. It's on our website. It's in the interview process. Once a team member is on board with us, we have an introductory meeting with them for internal training to share with them what this process is. It's a thirty-minute meeting that I host with all new hires within their first month. This is important because you can't abdicate this to their manager. The leader needs to share why this process is important. As you grow, you will find that your managers, although well-intentioned, will be more focused on technical training instead of cultural training. This is a good thing because it's not their job to create and establish the culture; it's yours!

After I introduce the concept to new hires, they schedule the PPF meeting with their manager after they've been with the organization for sixty days. The sixty-day number is based off experience. I wait sixty days for a couple of reasons:

1. They don't know what the opportunities are right off the bat. If they've only been with us for two weeks, they are still learning their role. It's not likely that they've put all of the

pieces together about where the business is going and what opportunities exist.

2. We know if someone is going to work out within sixty days. If they aren't a fit, I don't want you or your managers to waste time and energy on this conversation.

BEFORE THE PPF CONVERSATION

PPF FORM

PERSONAL GOALS

1 YEAR

3 YEARS

5 YEARS

PROFESSIONAL GOALS

1 YEAR

3 YEARS

5 YEARS

FINANCIAL GOALS

1 YEAR

3 YEARS

5 YEARS

Ahead of the PPF conversation, you should provide the team member with a PPF Form. This does not need to be fancy, but it should list the categories and time frames. The best time to send this document is after the introduction meeting during onboarding. That way, the team member will have a month to review and start jotting down ideas. It's not a requirement that everyone fills out each category. Ideally they do, but if they are struggling with a few of them, that's where you come in and guide the conversation. The form is merely a place for them to prep their ideas ahead of the conversation. When you introduce the form, don't be rigid. This process can be challenging for many team members because they've never gone through this before. You want to make them as comfortable as possible and ease their nerves.

DURING THE PPF CONVERSATION

This PPF conversation is not rocket science. It is literally as simple as sitting down with somebody and saying, "It's fantastic that you've joined our organization! I know you're two months in with us, and it's time for us to sit down and discuss your personal, professional, and financial goal planning because it's important to me and to this organization that you achieve your goals. As we grow, we want to align your goals with the business's goals so that we can win together. With that, let's get going! Walk me through your one-year personal goals." It's that simple.

Once you ask for their goals, write down what they're saying and make sure to be listening because it's going to be on you to ask great questions. You'll find that your team members will initially be vague. They might say that one of their one-year personal goals is to get in the best shape of their life. That's a great goal! But you need more context. This is where the SMART framework comes into play.

Here's the deal: you suck at asking questions. It's not necessarily your fault. There wasn't training in school as to how to be a great question asker, but that's about to change. When using the SMART framework, you'll be able to run through what questions to ask to get clarity quickly.

Here's what it stands for:

- S: specific. "What are you going to accomplish?"
- M: measurable. "How can you track the progress?"
- A: attainable. "Are you able to accomplish this goal?"
- R: relevant. "Why is this important to you?"
- T: timely. "When will you accomplish this goal?"

So if a team member shared the "get in the best shape of my life" goal with me, here are some questions I would ask before moving on to the next goal:

What activities are you going to do to get in shape (running, weights, yoga, etc.)? What's the best shape you've ever been in? How long ago was that? Why aren't you in that shape any longer? How often will you need to work out? Do you need to change your diet as well?

Depending on the answers, I would ask additional questions to ensure that I fully understand this goal. After I do, I'd move on to ask about the three-year goal and then start the question-asking process all over again.

After we've gone through all nine of the goals (one-, three-, and five-year goals for each PPF category), I ask the team member to send me their updated goals within the next twenty-four hours. Because people set goals in a variety of ways, I do provide a worksheet with the SMART framework because it's helpful to some people. I personally don't like to get that granular with each goal, but many of our team members thrive using that structure because it allows them to get clear on what they want.

When you're using the SMART framework in the conversation, don't literally ask, "How can we make that more specific?" or "Is that relevant to you?" You need to train yourself how to be naturally curious while knowing that the outcome is for you to help this person achieve these goals. The point of the conversation is to connect, not perfectly dial in every detail. But you do need the most important pieces. If your team member wants to have a weekly date night with their husband, you better ask what the husband's name is and be genuinely curious.

Once the conversation has taken place, it's the team member's responsibility to send their goals to the manager, ideally in the updated SMART format. The team member should then add these goals to their weekly One on One's to give their manager updates on where they are making progress and where they are stalling. I dive deep into the One on One process in the next chapter. In an ideal scene, incentive plans are established after the PPF conversation so that the team member can understand what they need to do to earn more money through selling your products and/or driving operational efficiencies. Incentive plans are always the trickiest part because it can be hard to craft them outside of sales. But we can do hard things, right? When it comes to the incentive plan, the goal is for every single team member in your organization to have full clarity on exactly what they need to do that day to make more money. The PPF conversation is the starting point to creating this incentive plan. Without clarity on their financial goals, it's hard to create targets for what activities they need to do that day to accomplish your goal. On the business's side, if you're not closing your books and reviewing your financials on a monthly basis, you will avoid creating non-sales incentive plans because you won't have confidence in the impact that the activity is having on the financials. Only lazy business owners don't review their financial statements on a monthly basis. Don't be lazy; get this discipline in.

WHAT NOT TO DO

After having my fair share of these conversations, I will give you some pro tips on what not to do. I have made every single one of these mistakes, and more, and I want to fast-track you so it doesn't take you eight years to be a pro.

DON'T MAKE IT IMPROMPTU

Let your team member prep in advance. It will make it go more smoothly. Don't just spring it on them when it's convenient for you. The more intentional you are in the setup, the smoother the process will be.

DON'T STAY IN THE OFFICE

Going to a Starbucks or a lunch spot that's around the corner will help get you the outcome you're looking for. Remember: the goal is to connect with your team members. Staying in your sterile, fluorescently lit office with work reminders everywhere and distractions isn't going to put either of you in the right frame of mind. Where do you go when you set and share your goals? I have a feeling it's not at your office desk.

DON'T RUSH

Book an hour for these meetings. That should give you plenty of time to work through all nine goals. If you only make them fifteen or thirty minutes, you're not going to be able to ask great questions and it will feel transactional. The fastest PPF I've ever done is forty-five minutes, but that is not standard. Do yourself a favor and commit to the hour.

DON'T JUMP RIGHT IN

When you start the meeting, don't just dive straight into asking about the goals. Start with the Vision. Why are you having this conversation? Why is this important for them and you? Spend two to three minutes introducing the value of the PPF process and sharing your commitment as a coach. This will properly frame the conversation and put the team member's nerves at ease. I can promise you that they will be nervous. Tapping into the "why" will help them understand the bigger context and ideally turn their nerves into excitement.

DON'T USE TECHNOLOGY

Using technology during these conversations is really a distraction. There are so many things that can come up. Since the goal is to really understand the goals, the team member won't know if you're paying attention or if you're on Instagram or sending a text. Bring a pen and piece of paper with you that you can take notes with. It's the only time I use paper these days, but it's an important step to give the team member confidence that they are your priority and have your full attention.

I can't tell you how many times I messed these conversations up, and it's taken me years to feel confident. I can assure you that your first few conversations will feel awkward and you will run into some hiccups. That's normal. Just keep pushing through and stay focused on why you're doing this: you're connecting with your team members and trying to understand what motivates them. If you keep that intention at the core of this process, the minutia doesn't matter.

CLIENT SUCCESS

"I own a construction company that had doubled in growth each of the previous three years from $0 to $2 million, $2 to $4 million, $4 to $8 million, and I was going for $8 to $16 million. I landed on $12 million, and that $12 million broke me, and the next year, we slipped back to $6 million. It was at this point that I found Cardone Ventures at one of the Grant Cardone Sales Boot Camps. I was literally at the boot camp looking to recharge. I was getting ready to run up the mountain again to achieve the goal of owning and operating a $100 million construction business. Thankfully, my wife, Leah, and I signed up to attend a Cardone Ventures event, and this is when I met Natalie.

While engaged in the Cardone Ventures training, it didn't take long before I realized that the feeling I had of my business being stuck in the first gear, kind of like a manual transmission car in first gear being revved to max capacity, was not normal. There was a technical business move that I was missing. I was trying to get to $100 million on my own without growing a results-oriented team of aligned, disciplined, and inspired people. How silly was my thinking? That is exactly when we went through the personal, professional, and financial (PPF) goal process, and I was completely blown away with how transactional my business philosophy had been. I had always hired people to do a job that I paid them for, whereas the PPF process had me taking the time to understand my team members' goals and desires in life.

During these PPF meetings, there were tears that were shed because no other leader had treated my team members this way before. As the leader of the team, we then were able to structure a plan for how our team members could hit their goals while the business was *hitting its goals. We were creating an aligned team that honestly transformed my home life because now I could spend time with my wife and our newborn daughter. I didn't have to work twenty-hour days every day of the week because I had team members that were inspired to put the extra work in. These were team members that held themselves accountable to the business's goals so they could hit their goals too! In 2021 we are on track to complete $22 million in sales, and my goal of operating a $100 million business is closer than ever before."*

—OLIVER FERNANDEZ, MCKENZIE CONSTRUCTION

AND SITE DEVELOPMENT

EMPLOYEE **DEVELOPMENT**

- ☑ ONBOARDING
- ☑ DAILY ALL-
  TEAM MEETINGS
- ☑ PPF GOALS
- ☑ **ONE ON ONES**
- ☐ QUARTERLY
  TEAM MEETINGS
- ☐ EMPLOYEE
  MATURITY MODEL

66 99

CHAPTER 11

ONE ON ONES

One on one meetings. Sure, it's not the sexiest topic, but it is a serious one. How serious? Well, at Cardone Ventures, we take One on One meetings so seriously that no one on our leadership team is eligible to receive incentive compensation unless they're conducting One on One meetings twice a month with every single one of their direct reports. That's right. Even if they're hitting all of their targets. There are no exceptions. That's how seriously we take One on One meetings.

Now, I understand that some of you might think that this policy in practice is a bit extreme, but I can assure you that it's not, and I'll tell you why. Without these twice monthly One on Ones, you've drastically increased the potential for everything to fall apart. As a people manager, there is so much crucial cultural *and* operational information to be gleaned from these conversations, from important business metrics pertaining to their specific role, to their personal, professional, and financial goals, their development plan, and so much more.

Isn't it worth your time to develop a bond and support their growth if it means that you're creating a high-performing team in the process? You don't just want *anyone* doing this job, right? You want your employees to be the best because ultimately their performance in their respective roles is what creates effectiveness. Your goal should be to build a team that is unstoppable, and conducting One on Ones, believe it or not, is one key way of achieving positive brand recognition. But what is more important than simply conducting these meetings is conducting them in the right way. Regular meetings with your direct reports, when done the *right* way, is the key to their success and yours.

THE PROCESS

No matter what size your business currently is, you should be conducting these meetings (as you are other aspects of the business) with your Vision statement in mind. Where do you intend to be ten years from now? Conduct and document your One on One meetings with *that* business in mind.

The first step is to create a One on One meeting template that is used across the organization by everyone. We'll dive into the agenda items below, but first we need to focus on how to roll this out to the entire team with uniformity.

One on Ones should be scheduled biweekly. I like to batch mine in thirty-minute increments on Thursday afternoons. Having them back-to-back allows me to block off that time to solely focus on my primary role with my team: being a coach. When they are sprinkled throughout the week, it's easy to become transactional in your communication. I want these meetings to be fruitful, and the best way to set this up for success is batching them together.

I place a recurring reminder the day before on my direct reports' calendars to send me their completed One on One forms. This gives me time to review them the following morning and get prepared for the conversation. I spend about thirty minutes reviewing them and making my own notes for areas I'd like to address. Earlier in my career, I didn't have this structure in place, and the One on Ones were all over the place. They became more of a social function with an emphasis on "catching up." I never knew how to redirect the conversation to the business initiatives, but that changed as soon as I introduced these forms. I've used this template for over five years now and have helped hundreds of businesses roll out this same structure for their meetings: it works like magic.

ONE ON ONE FORM

ACTIONS TAKEN:
(What action have you taken since our last 1:1?)

METRICS:
(How am I performing relative to my metrics?)

UPDATES AND IDEAS (What areas need to be addressed? What ideas do you have? Rank in order of priority and urgency)	RESPONSIBILITY (Who is responsible for achieving these actions?)	NOTES

PERSONAL, PROFESSIONAL, FINANCIAL GOALS:
(Updates and challenges)

PERSONAL	PROFESSIONAL	FINANCIAL
1 Year:	1 Year:	1 Year:
3 Years:	3 Years:	3 Years:
5 Years:	5 Years:	5 Years:

DEVELOPMENT PLAN:
(What action have you taken based on your Performance Review Development Plan?)

ACTION PLAN:
(What are the next steps and actions I will take after this meeting?)

EMPLOYEE'S SIGNATURE: _____ DATE: _____

MANAGER'S SIGNATURE: _____ DATE: _____

These are the essential areas you should cover in your One on One.

HEADING

Include the employee's name, their department, their manager's name, and the date. Only have two departments? Doesn't matter. Ultimately, your HR department will be organizing and storing this information for everyone's accountability. Don't skip this step.

ACTIONS TAKEN

Before moving on to new items, I start every One on One with reviewing the work that's taken place since our last meeting. It's incredibly frustrating to have a meeting where clear action items were established yet no progress was made afterward to complete them. This section should tie out to the previous One on One's "Action Plan" items. This is one way I reinforce our Core Values of Discipline and Accountability. If a team member says they will do something and don't, I have to address it in this meeting. One definition of leadership is one's ability to give and enforce orders. That can come across harsh, especially to new managers, but it's critical that you create a culture where leaders can establish what needs to get done and *enforce* that it actually happens. Without enforcing it, the environment becomes relaxed, and you'll sit back wondering why goals aren't being achieved.

METRICS

It's not by accident that the first order of business is reviewing each team member's metrics. This is one way I reiterate the

Core Value of Results. Effort is great, but I need to know how each person is performing relative to already established expectations. If they're falling short, what actions are they taking to rectify that? This brings up two scenarios: First, what if the role doesn't have metrics? Create them! There is no time like the present to button up the objectives and metrics of every role inside your organization. You are paying hourly for each contributor in your business, and when you hired them, there were specific business needs that drove you to make the post and find talent to help you. Every role should have clearly defined metrics that they have visibility into. The second scenario is if they have metrics but are underperforming. How do you handle this? Do you let them off the hook? Do you get frustrated? Ideally you are able to give them documented training to teach them how to function as a top performer in their role so that when performance issues take place, you can reference the documentation and provide the team member coaching in the area of struggle. By implementing this One on One process, you're making the commitment to your team and yourself that you're going to get the business organized and provide clarity to each team member so they can create success. You will be amazed at how quickly this transforms your culture.

UPDATES AND IDEAS

This is one of my favorite sections of the One on One because it tells you a lot about where the employee's head is. If they don't have any ideas, this is a problem. Like all businesses, I'm certain that your business has growth opportunities. I've never worked with a perfectly dialed-in business where everything worked flawlessly. There are *always* areas that can be improved. This spot in the form is the employee's chance to identify these areas that pertain to their role/ department. This section should be more informal, but request that they prioritize these ideas and make certain that these ideas about organizational improvement actually pertain to their department—otherwise, you're just throwing work into someone else's lap! I used to have these meetings, and by the end of them, I had a laundry list of items the team member put on my plate. This no longer happens. Sure, there are items that come up in this section that I end up needing to follow up on, but the majority of the time is spent with me approving new ideas and giving feedback on existing projects that are in the works. It's critically important for you to view yourself as a coach here. A coach doesn't run laps with the team. A coach is responsible for looking at the big picture, understanding the competition, and leveraging their experience to call the play. Stay focused on this as you go through this section.

PPF GOAL REVIEW

As I shared in the last chapter, the One on One is the place where the team member is sharing updates on their goals. They might not have an update for every meeting, but there should be an area where they are identifying wins or setbacks across their goals. This conversation should be led by the team member and guided by the manager. This space creates the opportunity to continue conversations as goals change, developments are made, and wins occur. It's important to get visibility into these areas with your top performers as they will need specific coaching on how to get to the next level.

DEVELOPMENT PLAN UPDATES

In Chapter 15 we'll dive into how the Development Plan is created during the performance review process, but it's important to note here that this is how you create focus on long-term behavior development and change. This should include four to six areas where the team member can improve their professional performance over the course of the year. Many team members I've worked with have the desire to become better at public speaking because they recognize that their lack of confidence in this area holds them back from leadership opportunities. Well, something like public speaking skills doesn't just happen overnight. It requires intentionality over a period of time to improve. These areas are addressed here. The team member uses this portion of their One on One to share with their manager what steps they are taking and where there's improvement. If they aren't taking any steps in these areas, it's the manager's job to call attention to this and frame why it's important to continue to chip away at these areas.

ACTION PLAN

This section is a takeaway for them to work on before your next meeting. They need to answer the question, "What are the steps and actions I will take after this meeting?" These are all the things that the team member documents and commits to so that when you next meet, they can answer the question, "What actions have you taken since our last One on One?"

AT CARDONE VENTURES

The One on One structure creates accountability for your

leaders to be coaches and your team members to be accountable to the outcome for their role. The accountability starts with the team member remembering to send the form ahead of the meeting. You both deserve the opportunity to prepare for this. No surprises. This is why we don't do these weekly at Cardone Ventures. It gives everyone a chance to take feedback, work to create a new result, and then report back on progress made.

Though I have been able to have a successful seventeen-minute One on One meeting, I recommend thirty minutes as a standard. Be very intentional about your time. It can go quickly. And these folks have chosen your organization to grow their careers. Be focused and be constructive in your feedback. Hold them accountable to their word. And make tough decisions if they aren't.

From an HR standpoint, this template allows you to document when you're working with an employee who is missing one of their metrics so that if a termination does need to occur, you have this series of events in black and white. This protects the organization. And it's not all for negative circumstances. Documentation is equally important for positive business and performance outcomes. In fact, it reinforces the kind of culture that you want to create.

It's taken me years to perfect this process, and I'm sure I'll continue to make improvements to it as Cardone Ventures grows. It helps you build great teams and a more successful business because it gets very specific about individual performance and accountability, which not only fosters great results, but also protects the integrity of your organization in the long run.

CLIENT SUCCESS

"The number one process for me was the One on Ones. At the People Essentials Workshop, you learn so much, and it's like a firehose. So when I came back, I listened to [Natalie's] podcasts just before I did the One on Ones with my people, and I was like, wow, what she did was just the right amount, and my people love it.

In the One on Ones, my team members tell me more ideas. Some of them have already hit some of their PPF goals, and now they're making new ones. Some of them that didn't really have any now have them, which makes it easier for us to pinpoint everything and get everybody in the same direction. I really enjoy doing them every other week.

Before the One on Ones, I had reviews set up at ninety days, six months, and once a year, but with One on Ones, you keep everybody focused. They know what their path is, they tell you what they want to do and where they want to go, and you get more ideas. You get ideas on a biweekly basis on how to improve their job, or they made an improvement that they're excited about sharing.

I think it's helped with retention overall. One of my goals was to find good people, and then keep them. So now I'm finding good people. If there is anything going on, they can bring it up in the One on Ones. That's a structured space to talk and get everything going the right direction so people stay. You don't have to retrain because they can train the next person, and then you can grow. You can scale your business. If people don't stay, you cannot scale your business. Natalie and Cardone Ventures have given us the tools, and we just have to implement them now and keep going."

—JULIE ALSTON, AERO & MARINE TAX PROFESSIONALS

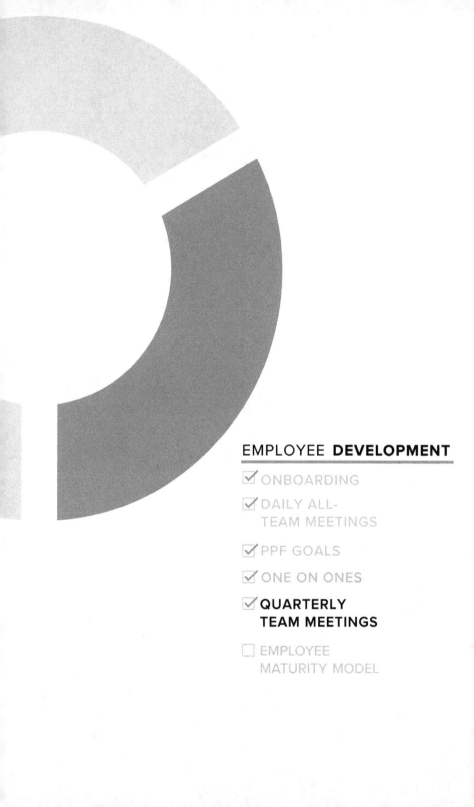

EMPLOYEE **DEVELOPMENT**

- ☑ ONBOARDING
- ☑ DAILY ALL-
  TEAM MEETINGS
- ☑ PPF GOALS
- ☑ ONE ON ONES
- ☑ **QUARTERLY
  TEAM MEETINGS**
- ☐ EMPLOYEE
  MATURITY MODEL

CHAPTER 12

QUARTERLY TEAM MEETINGS

Your quarterly team meetings (QTMs) are some of the most important meetings your organization can have. The QTM is something that I've participated in for the entirety of my career and has been a fixture of every business I've been a part of for as long as I can remember.

It's based on a very simple philosophy: you need your entire organization to be on the same page—moving in lockstep from their respective corners—as the business grows. When the business grows without this cross-departmental understanding, without the focus on seeing how your strategies and tactics and actions are interrelated, you run the risk of growing *and falling* apart.

No quarterly team meeting? You're creating a vacuum in your organization where communication will run amok. But an organization with intentionally led quarterly meetings? You have a place where, four times a year, you can communicate new, organization-wide changes and help your team feel confident in the direction of the company while also giving them something actionable that they can soon implement into their daily work.

The one caveat to this is "actionable": what you're communicating better be fully baked. This is not the place to fill the agenda with nonsense. This is about real, tangible movement in the organization. If you're not communicating clearly, your people, for better or worse, will fill in the blanks. Don't make that mistake. You want to be taken seriously. And being taken seriously means having a seriously thought-out plan. When it comes to your quarterly team meetings, that means having a seriously thought-out agenda.

QTM AGENDA

INTEGRATION POINTS

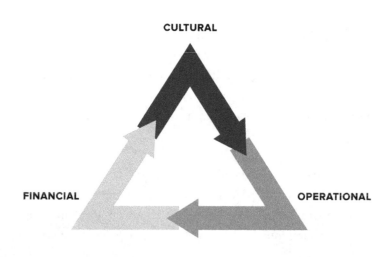

CULTURAL

FINANCIAL

OPERATIONAL

The three integration points of any business center around cultural, operational, and financial integration. Most businesses mess this cycle up. They focus on driving a financial result through operational levers and drive those processes into the culture. Strong organizations start with the culture and align it with the financial objective so they can create operational efficiencies. When a business starts the flow in reverse order, you'll find that there is a low sense of responsibility from the team members inside the environment. They weren't part of creating the operational efficiencies, so they don't have a high regard for fixing things when they break. For small business owners, the best way to get your team motivated and rallying behind a big financial target is to leverage their insights during the operational integration process. When you start with the culture, you will find a great deal of ease when making operational changes to hit a financial target.

When it comes to your QTM agenda, your presentation deck should flow in the cultural, operational, and financial order. This will help your team understand how their work is impacting the business and how interrelated their work is in order to achieve your Vision as a collective group.

CULTURAL

The topics that should be discussed during the cultural section of QTMs are: welcome; mission, vision, and values; company culture; and PPF goals celebration.

The beginning of this meeting is very similar to our daily all-team meetings in the sense that we're trying to create a feeling. We're welcoming people to work, and we're reminding them that we're all a part of something bigger than ourselves. But unlike the daily meeting, which focuses on the "right here, right now," the quarterly team meeting is centered around "where we've been, where we're going, and how we're getting there." This is the perfect opportunity to reiterate the Mission, Vision, and Core Values of the organization; aren't you glad you already did this work from the first few chapters?

We're using quarterly team meetings as a means of restating the Mission and Vision to remind everyone why we do the work we do and where we're going. This reminder is the best way to start this meeting because you're about to spend the next sixty to ninety minutes in the minutia. In all of the little things, and big things, the team does every day. These meetings can be difficult, especially when the business is not hitting its targets. When you start with the big picture, you're framing the conversation and setting up the dialogue that's to come.

After you've reviewed the Mission, Vision, and Values, it's time to cover some company culture topics—recognizing new hires and sharing the upcoming quarter's hiring plan. This is incredibly helpful if you currently have a strong culture because it gives you the opportunity to share with your team the roles you are looking to fill. Some of our very best team members are referrals from existing rock star team members. In this part of the presentation, I always highlight the incentive we pay if we do end up hiring the referral. Depending on your hiring needs, this can be anywhere from $250–$1000.

If you have things like book clubs, exercise challenges, and team holiday events, this is the place to share those updates. It's important to create ways for your teams to get closer, support each other, and grow together. This is the perfect place to share what's upcoming for the next three months.

The last element of the cultural portion of our meeting is one of the most important: supporting the achievement of personal, professional, and financial goals. In this section, you're able to showcase and highlight team members who have achieved their goals. It gives them the public praise they deserve, shows your commitment to the company Mission, and can be used as inspiration for others to achieve their goals. When you create a culture where people are winning, you need to promote the wins.

OPERATIONAL

In the operational portion of the meeting, this is your time to discuss performance and realign the entire organization in the pursuit of your goals. One way I suggest you do this is by delivering departmental updates. Each department head or key teammate takes a slide to discuss performance, communicate the tactics they used to meet or exceed their quarterly KPIs, or, if the team is falling short of their goal, speak to the commitments that are being made in order to get things back on track. This is also a place for leadership to communicate the next quarter's priorities, as well as introduce any new initiatives that will soon be released and supported by the team.

As I said earlier, this is where you need to be extra careful. New initiatives are not about filling space. Only introduce new initiatives to the company if there's an airtight strategy in place. You do not want to put yourself or anyone else in your leadership team in a space where they're perceived as all talk and no action.

FINANCIAL

The financial update is about as simple as it sounds. Your team needs to understand the financial health of the company. Everybody is responsible for it. What is the budget to actual of each month in the quarter? Is the business healthy? If it's not, again, what is the strategy for stabilizing and fostering growth? If the business is healthy, how are we using that momentum to create even more growth? Financial transparency inside your organization will be critical to your long-term success. After completing this section, go straight into a Q&A.

Q&A AND CLOSING

This is where you learn how to force engagement. I know, force sounds a little strong, but I've been in this situation in previous years, and I'd be lying if I said this portion can't be a little miserable if you *don't* force engagement. Now, when I open the floor up for Q&A, I am not saying, "Does anyone have any questions?" Nope, what I'm saying now is, "What questions do you have?" because I know people have questions. They're just afraid to speak.

If somebody doesn't immediately ask me a question, I simply say to the group that we are not getting off the call until there have been at least five great questions asked. And you know what? People start asking questions! It forces engagement. And we're all better off for it. You don't need to draw this portion out. Give it about ten to fifteen minutes, and then conclude the meeting.

I can promise you that these meetings are a game changer. Just commit. They don't have to be perfect. But you do need to be clear. You need to show your team that you're a serious leader and that you're committed to their growth, because that's what will help foster their commitment to the company's growth. From then on, if you stick with it, they'll only get better.

AT CARDONE VENTURES

We have a saying that "the only emotion allowed in business is celebration." Sometimes these meetings don't exactly share results that are worth celebrating. When you're not hitting your numbers, this meeting can feel like a dread, and you will likely consider scrapping it altogether. The quarters you are off are the *exact* opportunities that the quarterly team meeting is built for. This meeting forces you and the team to confront where the business is at and come up with a plan. These are the moments when true entrepreneurialism is exposed.

In the first quarter of 2021, we were off from our target by 37 percent, and you could feel the heaviness during the meeting. It's painful to fumble out of the gate when you have big plans for the year. The meeting was myopically focused on the three KPIs we needed to focus on to make up for Q1 in Q2. There was clarity, and every team knew what they needed to do to close the gap. In Q2, we entirely made up the 37 percent from Q1 and ended up being 11 percent over target. The QTM was electric! The energy was palpable and the team celebrated. After the meeting, I called our exec team to congratulate them on an incredible quarter. Each of them commented on how incredible the meeting was and how excited their teams were.

The next day, I got a resignation from a team member who had been with us for two weeks. She said that we expected too much, and this wasn't a "cultural" fit for her. My response? If hitting our company's goals so that our teams accomplish *their* goals isn't a cultural fit for her: good riddance.

EMPLOYEE **DEVELOPMENT**

- ☑ ONBOARDING
- ☑ DAILY ALL-
  TEAM MEETINGS
- ☑ PPF GOALS
- ☑ ONE ON ONES
- ☑ QUARTERLY
  TEAM MEETINGS
- ☑ **EMPLOYEE
  MATURITY MODEL**

CHAPTER 13

EMPLOYEE MATURITY MODEL

CREATE CAREERS—NOT JOBS

No one wants a job. The definition of a job is "a paid position of regular employment." The word "regular" should be repulsive to you because there's nothing that can be regular in creating a transformational business, especially not your team members. Every role within your business should be viewed as a career-building opportunity, and the way to set that up is through the Employee Maturity Model. You're likely more familiar with the term "career pathing."

Career pathing is a process that team members use to chart a course within an organization for their career path and development. It involves understanding what competencies, knowledge, skills, and experience are necessary for an employee to progress their career through promotions and/or departmental transfers. It requires an employee to take an honest look at their career goals and make a plan to obtain what is necessary, for each of these areas, to carry out their career path.

An Employee Maturity Model is different than traditional career pathing. If you're expecting your team members to path their career, you're leaving it up to them to create what's possible. That shouldn't be their job, and you shouldn't rely on your team members to be go-getters when it comes to this. How are they supposed to map their career development without understanding what you're looking for? It's your responsibility to show them what's possible because most team members don't know.

Think back to your first job. Did you know what opportunities existed for your advancement? My guess is you were stuck in an organization and you thought that your only responsibility there was to complete your role. Initially, it is your job to do the role you were hired for. The idea isn't that a new team member starts and within weeks moves into a different role. They need to become great at the role that they are in first, demonstrating that they're able to be a top performer in that role. But if you don't give them the picture for why being a top performer is important, it's not likely they're going to get there and stay there. So why wait until they choose to be disengaged to start talking to them about the opportunity that exists?

With the Employee Maturity Model, you're taking the guesswork out of the equation. You're not hoping that a team member or two are going to take this responsibility on themselves. You're going to put it in front of every one of them. You're going to let them know that you're willing to give them the tools and resources, opportunity, and knowledge to add value to themselves so that they can add value to the business. That way, as the business grows, they grow.

As part of the onboarding plan, I spend thirty minutes with every new team member to walk them through this. I host these meetings once per month and include anyone who has been with us for less than thirty days. It's important that team members hear there is room for growth before having their PPF conversations. The Employee Maturity Model document gives a guide for the conversation as they can set their professional and financial goals around it.

What gives the Employee Maturity Model credibility is real-life examples of team members who have moved up. If you are a startup, your primary focus with the first team members you bring on is creating these examples. You don't give your first employee a VP title when they are making $75K per year. Follow the proper structure; at that base, they should be in the manager or director category, and you drive them toward the objectives, competencies, and metrics they need to hit to get a promotion. If you have many team members already who have followed a maturity path with you, share that with new team members! Let them know where John started and what it took for him to get where he is now.

The Employee Maturity Model, EMM for short, is comprised of the following categories.

ME VERSUS WE BREAKDOWN

In Chapter 10, I broke down the difference in ME versus WE roles for you, and a similar description is the starting point of the EMM. It's important for your team to understand this concept early on in their employment with you. You're results-oriented and want them to be as well. The steps you're going to lay out through the EMM *is* the process for moving from being a ME contributor to a WE contributor.

PAY BANDS

I believe it's imperative to put financial opportunity that's associated with growth in front of every team member. Every person on your team should be highly incentivized by making more money if your goal as a business owner is to grow your business. There are certainly people out there who are not financially motivated; let your competitors hire them. You should reserve seats in your organization for the financially motivated and then show them what's possible for them through working with you.

POSITION COMPETENCIES

Once you have established the pay range for each position in the organization, the next step is the breakdown of competencies required at each position level. We all inherently understand that a CMO makes more than a marketing coordinator, but what is the actual qualitative difference between these two roles? *That* is what gets documented here. The description of the expectation at each position will help educate and bring awareness to pay differences. It will also create a baseline for the team members in more senior positions. When you set clear requirements for every position type, there's understanding of the contribution you're expecting.

PAY BANDS

When it comes to establishing your organization's pay bands, it's important to set up the structure to reflect that more responsibility, results, and leadership is what creates additional pay within your organization. It sounds as if this might just be a given, but in most organizations, it's not. If someone joins the team as a coordinator, elevating to the responsibility of a manager should come as a reward after they've increased their value and commitment to the organization. From a financial stand-point, a coordinator is not as valuable as a manager because they don't have the skills and experience to solve manager-level problems and create value that's commensurate with being a manager. It becomes a skills game, and how easy is it to teach skills? Pretty easy if somebody is willing to learn. And the only reason that somebody becomes willing to learn something is if their goals are in alignment with having to put that energy and effort into it, taking up something new, going through the steps to figure it out, practicing, and then becoming an expert at that thing.

Many business owners get caught up and concerned with the idea of sharing pay bands with all of their team members. And to that I say: you should always be confident sharing pay bands in your organization. It defines the value each role holds because it's tied to all of the things that a person in that position should contribute to the entity. So as you're thinking of these pay bands, it's important to remember that you're painting a picture and raising what they believe is possible by showing them that if they add the skillset, if they do the work, if they put in the time it's going to take to improve from a financial standpoint, they will become better off, but they have to actually get the skills and then create the result that's necessary.

And so if you have hesitation around publishing your pay bands, I would ask that you reconsider what your role is for your team members. As the leader of the business, you already have cre-ated a picture for the entity: your Vision states where you're going. But everybody inside that entity needs to understand how they benefit. Just having financial targets for the organization and publishing them is a great start. But the next level of pay bands really makes it real for people that if they focus and they put their energy into developing themselves, they will be financially rewarded for the results.

When you're coming up with your pay bands, the first place to start is by looking at existing performers. If you currently have a coordinator or manager or senior manager, or a handful of them, you already know what the position generates for the business and how much they cost. This can be a great starting point. If it's a brand new role and you don't have somebody in these more senior-level positions, I would highly recommend doing some online research and getting a better understanding of what pay for those positions in your city looks like. There can certainly be a variation from city to city of the value between different position levels, so doing some research will keep your compensation packages competitive. This will be helpful for you in the negotiation process.

PAY BANDS

WE ROLES

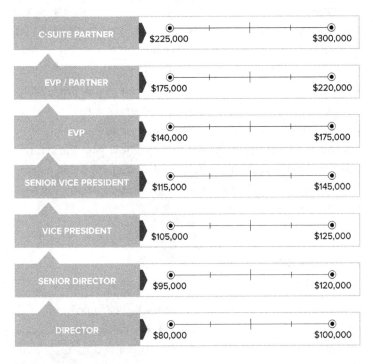

Role	Min	Max
C-SUITE PARTNER	$225,000	$300,000
EVP / PARTNER	$175,000	$220,000
EVP	$140,000	$175,000
SENIOR VICE PRESIDENT	$115,000	$145,000
VICE PRESIDENT	$105,000	$125,000
SENIOR DIRECTOR	$95,000	$120,000
DIRECTOR	$80,000	$100,000

ME ROLES

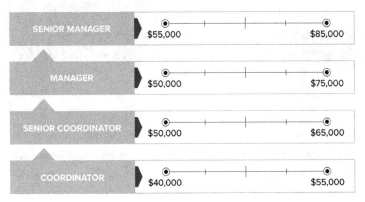

Role	Min	Max
SENIOR MANAGER	$55,000	$85,000
MANAGER	$50,000	$75,000
SENIOR COORDINATOR	$50,000	$65,000
COORDINATOR	$40,000	$55,000

Another consideration in establishing pay bands is your industry. If your team requires specialized training, stick to industry norms for position name conventions and pay range. It will be helpful to you as you post jobs and are sourcing candidates because you're looking for somebody with a specific set of requirements and experience. I often see business owners get creative with their title structures in order to differentiate themselves. I'm all for differentiation, but if you're having difficulty getting the right people to apply to your posts, this is likely why. My recommendation would be to differentiate yourself in another category: your proven process, how you market, the way you service your clients. Creating strange roles that no one has heard of doesn't make your organization more desirable to top talent, it confuses them.

POSITION BREAKDOWN
BEHAVIORAL COMPETENCIES

There are core behavioral competencies at each position level, and as you add more and more team members, you will notice that there are commonalities across position levels. Yes, a marketing coordinator and an operations coordinator have differing role objectives, technical competencies, and metrics, but there will be an underlying set of behavioral competencies that span across both roles. These are what you document in the "coordinator" position for behavioral competencies in the Employee Maturity Model.

In the EMM, you need to make clear that these behavioral competencies are a requirement as part of the pathway for promotion. Developing a competency in any area does not happen overnight. Now, I will never say you have to be in the organization for years and years to be able to get a promotion because I do believe that you do not have to be around for a significant amount of time to create true value in an organization. However, as a team member starts to hit their role-specific objectives, technical competencies, and metrics, the behavioral competencies that they are developing are equally important and sometimes take longer. Examples of behavioral competencies include the following:

- Assumes responsibility for the results of own actions and their impact on the team
- Plans ahead for upcoming problems or opportunities and takes appropriate action; recognizes and acts upon opportunities
- Demonstrates resilience against challenges and obstacles
- Holds self and others accountable for making principled decisions; addresses unethical behaviors head-on
- Makes clear and effective presentations
- Can quickly find common ground and solve problems for the good of all
- Understands how to separate and combine tasks into efficient workflows
- Provides original ideas and adds value during brainstorming sessions
- Can negotiate skillfully in tough situations with both internal and external groups

You don't just become a great communicator overnight. You don't learn how to manage your stress through just a couple of weeks of focus. It's a process where you only see progress over time. But these things are required in order to be fully competent in your position in the organization. To illustrate this, a senior finance manager could be a top performer at his role. He's a QuickBooks wiz, can create a financial model with accuracy, and closes out the books on time every month. But he gets incredibly nervous talking in front of people and can't make presentations that get to the point. This behavioral competency of making clear and effective presentations would prevent him from being promoted to a director of finance. Even if he is the best senior finance manager we've ever had, his inability to communicate is currently holding him back, and he needs to spend time developing this competency and overcoming his nerves because it takes away from the business objectives.

Starting with entry-level positions, you should add suggested reading to each position in your EMM. Leveraging books is an easy way to enhance your team's behavioral competencies at every level of your organization. Just as you're reading this book right now, I'm certain that you've read dozens of books that changed your perspective and enhanced your ability to problem solve or taught you leadership philosophies. This is different than the required reading in your onboarding plan; that should be viewed as baseline reading, whereas this suggested reading is not mandatory but can serve as a guide for team members who are looking for how to develop but aren't certain of how to do that. Anything you've found to be helpful on your development journey, you should add in. Some of my favorites include:

- *Be Obsessed or Be Average* by Grant Cardone
- *Start with Why* by Simon Sinek
- *17 Indisputable Laws of Teamwork* by John Maxwell
- *Good to Great* by Jim Collins
- *3 Feet from Gold* by Sharon Lechter

KNOWLEDGE

Knowledge can be broken down into organization, industry, trends, and competition. What do your top performers need to know about the organization, the industry that you're in, trends for their department, or your competition that will give you an edge and set them up for adding greater value? The organization knowledge is more important at entry-level roles. Ensuring that everyone knows how to explain your business model, the key products/services you sell, and how the organization operates is critically important. Once that's established, ideally in the coordinator and manager positions, you'll need to place less of an emphasis on the organization and more of an emphasis on trends for that function. Being up to speed on trends will be important for your middle management and senior management positions because they need to continue to increase their technical competency and become great leaders within their function.

Your VPs and C-Suite's responsibility is tied to the organization's position in the market, viability, and long-term success, so their knowledge of your competition and the industry will determine how well they're able to add overarching value to the organization.

MANAGER VS SENIOR MANAGER

	MANAGER	**SENIOR MANAGER**
JOB DESCRIPTION	**JOB DESCRIPTION: MANAGER** Objectives Competencies Metrics	**JOB DESCRIPTION: SENIOR MANAGER** Objectives Competencies Metrics
BOOKS	Be Obsessed or Be Average by Grant Cardone Start with Why by Simon Sinek 10X Rule by Grant Cardone	17 Indisputable Laws of Team Work by John Maxwell Good to Great by Jim Collins 3 Feet from Gold by Sharon Lechter
KNOWLEDGE	Organization Industry Trends Competition	Organization Industry Trends Competition

PROMOTION

So how do you use the EMM in the promotion process?

PROMOTION EQUATION

MASTERY OF JOB DESCRIPTION

EMM
(BEHAVIORAL COMPETENCIES + KNOWLEDGE)

BUSINESS NEED

=

PROMOTION

MASTERY OF JOB DESCRIPTION

Because I know how good a job you did after Chapter 6 dialing in your job descriptions, you are going to breeeeeze through this section…right? I sure hope so because it's the foundation for creating successful role comparisons. If you haven't completed this yet, please help me understand: what are you waiting for? Hammer them out. It shouldn't take more than a weekend to get the objectives, competencies, and metrics for every role. Bring the team into the office and knock this out. If you don't do it all at once, it's one of those projects you can perpetually put on the back burner just for it never to get fully cooked. Stop making excuses and take this seriously. Target this weekend and just get it done. I'm a huge proponent of taking time out of the equation. Once you know something is critical to your success (and I promise you this is), don't add time between now and getting it done. Just do it.

With the completed job descriptions, you've now established your base requirement: if you've hired an operations manager and you have the objectives, competencies, and metrics listed out, that is the minimum requirement for that role to output. So take a look at it and ask, "If this is the baseline for an operations manager, what would the requirements for a senior operations manager be?" What do they need to know? What results would they need to achieve? What technical capabilities do they have that the manager does not?

Determining the differentiation between these two roles should be your priority, especially when your target is to attract and retain high achievers. If you don't have the baseline job description and they don't know what they're currently being measured against to become a top performer, you're going to have a very hard time aligning their goals and pushing them to contribute at the senior manager level, much less a director level.

Objectives

Let's apply what we learned about the job description in Chapter 6 to how you use it in the promotion process. The team member should be able to competently complete all objectives and ensure each process that's associated with the role objectives is documented. If they aren't currently documented, the team member needs to understand that the documentation process is a big opportunity for them to be able to move up in the organization. But they only get to be responsible for process documentation once they've proven that they are a top performer and are hitting their metrics. The documentation process is what's needed to set the next person up for success who would be responsible for taking on that role.

This helps you as the business owner actually scales and grows because you're empowering your team to solve the business's current duplication problems and you're reinforcing how important documentation is. This way, you're able to teach them how to add value through the documentation, and they'll understand that they are going to then be responsible for training somebody new to achieve the same results they did.

Competencies

Ideally when you hired the team member, they already possessed the competencies listed in the job post. If these technical competencies needed to be developed, the team member should have been on the lower end of the pay scale. The more you have to train team members from a technical standpoint, the less monetary value they have when they walk in the door because you're spending time and resources getting them prepped to do the job. Once their technical competencies meet the requirements of the role, it's important for them to know what the technical competencies are for the senior position so they can start working on acquiring those skills.

Metrics

From a metrics standpoint, they need to be the top performer. So whatever those metrics are that you've established, they have to be in the top 10 percent of hitting those metrics and do it on a consistent basis. It is not just once that somebody needs to be able to hit a metric so that they can then get promoted. No, they have to show a track record of consistency. One of the reasons that this is important is when you're adding new team members, they have to know that it's not just a one-time thing that their manager was able to achieve. Their new leader, who used to be in the role, has to have a track record of hitting the metric consistently so the team member's belief in their own ability to duplicate that result stays high. It will certainly increase the belief of the new team member because they know it's actually possible. It's not just luck. It wasn't just a good month or a good quarter. It happened consistently over a period of time.

BUSINESS NEED

It's unfortunate, but a reality, that a team member can hit the requirements defined in their job description and focus on the EMM areas that they need in order to get promoted to the next role in the organization but still not get promoted. Because if the business isn't growing for them to be able to be paid more money, they actually have not added true value.

I want this to sink in because in senior-level roles, it becomes about creating true quantifiable value that allows for you to be paid more. Now, that person could choose to leave, and they could get paid more at another organization for the skills, competencies, and knowledge that they have. And that's a risk that you take. In an ideal scene, you're able to tie their development to true value because if they decide to move on to another entity without adding more clients or doing something that adds true business value to the organization, eventually they're going to get stuck there too because they haven't learned the skillset that it's going to take to grow something.

So this shouldn't be something that you get scared of or nervous about, but you should be thinking of how to structure this entire model to incentivize the right things. Not just development for development's sake. I was at a conference where a client of ours said that they paid money for team members to read business books. She asked me if I thought this was a good idea, and I shared that I believe in recognizing effort, but rewarding results. I will recognize and be appreciative that you've put all this time into yourself, but I'm not actually going to reward you unless there is a result that is tied to true value.

The EMM's goal is to create a systematic structure that guides every team member to add value to themselves, which benefits the business and helps them achieve their personal, professional, and financial goals. I do want to caveat that as much as you can try to create the perfect structure, there can be any number of factors that lead to why someone is promoted: new product development, the departure of a team member, a reorg. The list goes on and on. The EMM won't cover *every* scenario, but 90 percent of your promotions should be in alignment with your documented EMM process. Your job is to remove as much of the subjective criteria as possible to be able to set the standard across the organization for who gets promoted and why. No one enjoys jumping through political corporate hoops or being passed up for a promotion due to nepotism or playing favorites. The EMM allows you to have a clear-cut set of criteria. It's up to you to ensure it's used and perpetuated as your team gets bigger.

All promotions should be tied to a result that's been achieved. This is why I favor the "result" Core Value; it can (and should) be used as a reason for someone to be promoted through the performance review process that we'll get into in the next chapter. This truly reinforces that you hire, *reward*, and fire using your Core Values. But results are only part of the equation. Many times over, I've worked with business owners who have a rock star team member who consistently creates results, but they steamroll other people and are reckless to the culture. *This* is where you point to the behavioral competencies in the EMM that are required for promotion. Their bullish ways are the exact thing that need to be course-corrected and have likely held them back their entire life. You have to refuse to put these types of people in leadership positions, even if they do generate a significant amount of revenue for your business or your clients love them.

One of my favorite Grant Cardone quotes is "Your assets become your liabilities." Your superstar employee will become a liability when you are so dependent on them that you've lost leverage in being able to create boundaries in the environment. Don't set yourself, and your business, up for failure in this way. Make it clear what gets rewarded and what doesn't.

Results are an important part of the equation but not everything. All the other pieces need to be clearly articulated in your Employee Maturity Model. I've had five years of experience with delivering and utilizing the EMM, and it works with all variations of employee challenges and personality difficulties that you will most certainly come up against while growing your business. If set up correctly, it will incentivize the personal, professional, and financial achievement of your team members while creating a high-performing culture and substantial business growth.

CLIENT SUCCESS

"Our biggest success has come through the Employee Maturity Model, where we have completely outlined how to take someone from an entry role through a top executive role and even partner. We have found that the only way to have a bigger and better business is with the help of a great team. With the Employee Maturity Model, our team knows exactly what is expected of them to move up in our organization. Our team can now see the road map to not only how the company grows but how they can grow within the company and achieve their personal, professional, and financial goals. I can't say enough about how much we have learned and gained from the information [Natalie] has provided. We are on a bright and exciting new chapter in our business because of Natalie. We wish we had only had this knowledge and implemented it years ago. Thank you."

—KELAN LIPAROTO, ADVANTAGE PHYSICAL THERAPY

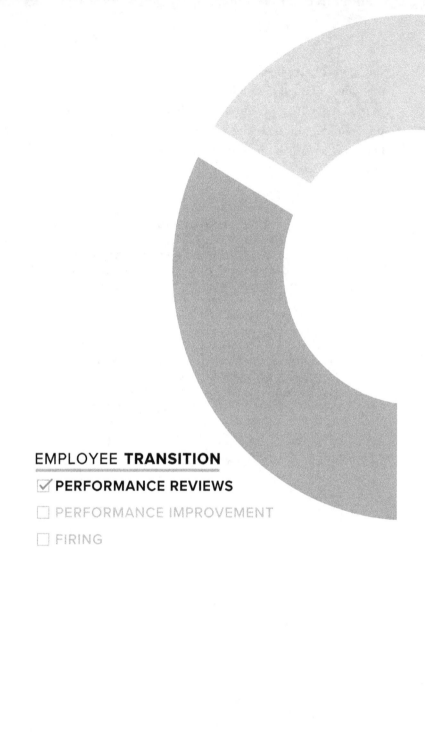

EMPLOYEE **TRANSITION**

☑ **PERFORMANCE REVIEWS**

☐ PERFORMANCE IMPROVEMENT

☐ FIRING

CHAPTER 14

PERFORMANCE REVIEWS

Do you remember in Chapter 4 when we discussed using your Core Values for hiring, rewarding, and firing? I bet you were thinking, "I get the hiring and firing piece but how do you use them to reward?" Look no further: the performance review is the *reward* process. The performance review process is an essential way to utilize your Core Values in your culture because when you think of your employee touchpoints, the hiring portion of the Core Values only lasts during the interview and on the firing side; ideally you don't have to make it there. The step for truly defining your culture with your Core Values is the reward process.

The foundation of the process is this: you should be rewarding your team members for the behavior and outcomes you've established. It's that simple. There shouldn't be dozens of things that are rewarded in your environment. If showing up on time or accuracy is important for you, your Core Values should clearly state that, and you should be recognizing and rewarding people when they demonstrate those characteristics in your environment.

I often get significant pushback from our clients because they are convinced that they need to keep certain Core Values that they already have in place. A handful of them include domination, winning, and innovation, but the review process makes those Core Values challenging because they have to be *workable*.

That is the difference between a good Core Value and a bad Core Value: is it actually workable? Can you use it to promote and continue to have people evolve using the words that you've chosen? This is why I have my approved Core Values and others that are on the "no" list. I have prepped and conducted over 250 performance reviews and can tell you what works and what doesn't because one of the biggest challenges is having these words span across every role. Can the CFO and the assistant be assessed on the same Core Values because there's enough of a gradient? A word like discipline is ideal because it's a characteristic that evolves and has infinite potential. Your discipline today is very different than your discipline when you first started your career. You've gotten better and better, but there's no point in time where you will be 100 percent disciplined in every single thing that you do for the rest of your life. The same goes with the Core Value of accountable. When a team member is junior and first starting out, they can be accountable for getting their tasks done, checking off a checklist, and ensuring that they're doing every single thing that they have been assigned. But as they grow in their role and transition into different responsibilities, the accountability will shift to ensuring that everything in the department is happening in the way that it should be happening. They're now accountable to a larger role and needing to address and confront team members who aren't being accountable.

Your Core Values don't have to be perfect, and trust me when I tell you that this performance review process will really put them to the test. I would recommend that you stick with what you have and learn the same way I did: try it. As soon as you go through a full performance review cycle, it will be clear to you what criteria are missing that you'll want to add to your list. There might be a few. Make note of it while it's happening and then make a change. No one ever said you have to have the same Core Values forever. If something isn't working, switch it out. They are *yours* to use and define your culture.

THE PROCESS

I recommend implementing a performance review annually at the end of the year. Many organizations try to do this twice per year, others once every quarter. There's nothing wrong with giving feedback more often; however, if you have implemented the One on One structure I recommend in Chapter 11, an annual performance review is sufficient. We do annual reviews for two reasons:

1. We tie promotions to our performance reviews, and doing it once per year gives the business financial predictability. When you promote randomly, you're going to have a difficult time forecasting correctly at the beginning of the year.
2. The team has an entire year to hit their metrics, work on areas in the Employee Maturity Model, and focus on their areas of growth.

TRANSPARENCY

Ideally, you are sending out a document to your whole team telling them what the performance review process is going to look like so it is not a surprise. The last thing that you want to do is surprise your team members as to what they are being graded on. Put yourself in your team's shoes: I know in July that come December, I'm either going to get a promotion or I'm not going to get a promotion. I'm going to get feedback that I need to fix something based on this set of criteria. Well, why wouldn't you give me that criteria before the test already arrived? Why don't you allow me to study and do some prep work?

CONSISTENCY

I find that there are two types of business owners. One gives too much feedback. Every single day there is something that's being done wrong, and the owner is getting upset about it. These types of organizations have high turnover because the team constantly feels attacked. The other type of business owner doesn't give any feedback. Somebody could be working in that organization for years and years and years, but never actually receive direct feedback about how things could get better.

In either scenario, without a performance review process, you're not setting up the organization to scale. You have gotten by with the way you give feedback for now, but I can promise you that it won't work as you grow and add team members because you can't build your business around you. Imagine how difficult that gets when you grow to forty team members and have managers who are managing team members. All of the sudden you're not the one that's responsible any longer for all of the feedback that's being given. And if you're bad at giving feedback currently, why would your future managers be more committed to having hard conversations than you are?

I've never found that managers are better at giving feedback than the business owner is. The owner really does set the tone. You have to remember this as you grow and scale your team because it's going to be your responsibility to teach your managers how to give feedback in a way that really is constructive and that helps their team members learn and grow. This process is built for that because it creates consistency. The first year, you should have significant oversight into this process. You should sit with new managers and have them watch you give a review, then let them do it and give them feedback. You can't assume they're going to do it well their first time. It might take ten before they're comfortable and doing a great job with it. That's okay. This process truly does set the whole team up for success if it's followed properly.

PREPARATION

I highly recommend you create a document with the content below that lives on a shared drive for your whole team to access at any time. Other things in this drive could include One on One forms, the employee handbook, policies, etc. Before scheduling the reviews, I'll send this in an email to every team member one month before with the dates for every step.

STEP 1: TEAM PREPARATION

Each person will fill out the Core Values assessment - employee form (this will also be attached in the meeting invite from your manager). Be sure to set aside thirty minutes to focus your efforts on filling this form out. Each team member will send their completed form to their manager one week before the scheduled performance review.

Form Elements

Page 1: Your Core Values Alignment Assessment

CORE VALUES
ASSESSMENT

INSPIRATIONAL
\+   O   –
☐ ☐ ☐

DISCIPLINED
\+   O   –
☐ ☐ ☐

ACCOUNTABLE
\+   O   –
☐ ☐ ☐

RESULTS-ORIENTED
\+   O   –
☐ ☐ ☐

TRANSPARENT
\+   O   –
☐ ☐ ☐

INTENTIONAL
\+   O   –
☐ ☐ ☐

We want you to select your alignment as "positive," "neutral," or "negative." By selecting positive, you should be able to provide a strong example of full alignment. Neutral represents alignment, yet you wouldn't have a solid example. Negative would indicate no alignment to that Core Value.

CORE VALUES ASSESSMENT

STRENGTHS

CORE VALUE

EXAMPLE(S)

CORE VALUE

EXAMPLE(S)

OPPORTUNITIES

CORE VALUE

EXAMPLE(S)

CORE VALUE

EXAMPLE(S)

Strengths—what is going really well?

1. Use this section to highlight your Core Values alignment, the wins for this year, and your key contributions. This could include key achievements, goals met, project completions, improvements over prior year, professional milestones, or anything else of note.
2. Be prepared to discuss your ideas for carrying over the positive momentum into the next year.
3. Don't be shy. If you are proud of an accomplishment, it is worth sharing with your manager during your review! Don't hesitate to be your own advocate.

Opportunities—what are some challenges?

1. Use this section to identify any results or outcomes that may have fallen short of expectations. Those expectations may have been your own, your manager's, or another stakeholder's such as a peer or client.
2. This is often an uncomfortable part of the discussion, but the purpose isn't to dwell on what went wrong. By acknowledging when things did not go as planned and engaging in open, honest reflection, you are empowering yourself to learn from it and move on. To make the most of the conversation with your manager, try testing the limits of your comfort zone by opening up a little more than normal.
3. There is no "wrong" way to complete this section. Be prepared to discuss what you have learned or would have done differently with the benefit of hindsight. Approaching it with objectivity, humility, and a plan for moving forward will make this discussion a productive one.

Partnering for Success

The purpose of this section is to provide a space for reflection on how you and your manager can continue to work together to help you achieve your goals and ensure that the team is meeting its objectives.

1. What additional support can your manager provide to help you achieve the next level of success in your role and career at our company?
2. This question is intentionally open-ended. By this point in your preparation efforts, you should have a better idea of additional items to discuss with your manager.
3. Make sure any feedback you provide is delivered in a constructive, respectful manner. Keep it forward-looking and focused on solutions.
4. Be mindful of your team's priorities and objectives for the next year and beyond. How does the support you are requesting enable you to help the team be more successful?
5. It is possible that your manager will have a different viewpoint on your request. Be prepared to discuss a variety of possible solutions.

Top PPF Goals

Identify the one to three PPF goals that are top of mind for you right now. Indicate the status of the goal(s) and provide any relevant notes or comments about what is needed for achievement. It is important that your PPF goals remain a part of the ongoing conversation between you and your manager. Your annual review is a timely occasion to discuss your progress on these goals and the impact your contributions to the team might have on helping you move closer to reaching them.

STEP 2: PERFORMANCE REVIEW MEETING

1. Your manager will be filling out the Core Values assessment - manager form about you from their perspective. The only difference between the forms is that your manager won't have the "Partnering for Success and Top PPFs" section and theirs will have "Overall Performance Ratings."

2. During the meeting, your manager will share their form and your form to review areas of alignment and feedback. Your manager will also cover the elements of the Development Plan template for you to complete after the meeting. This development plan will establish the four to six areas of professional growth for the upcoming year.

STEP 3: FINALIZE DEVELOPMENT PLAN

1. Complete the development plan and schedule a follow-up meeting within one week to review and finalize your plan with your manager.

HOW TO MAKE YOUR REVIEW SUCCESSFUL

1. Be prepared. The more thoughtful effort you put into completing the Core Values assessment, the greater the likelihood that you will have a meaningful, productive review conversation with your manager.

2. Don't be afraid to ask your peers for feedback in any of the areas that will be covered in the review.

3. Keep an open mind: even if you disagree with what you are hearing, remember that there is a reason your manager has chosen to share this feedback with you. Try to avoid making assumptions, and do your best to ask questions in order to better understand where he or she is coming from.

4. Do not panic or be discouraged if your manager's eval-

uation of you differs from your Core Values assessment. Use the remainder of the meeting as an opportunity to ask questions and get on the same page with your manager about what is expected. There is never a bad time to get things back on track.

TIPS FOR SUCCESS
DON'T CLOUD YOUR REVIEW

Even though your team members will send you their assessments ahead of time, I highly recommend that you don't read them before you fill out your assessment of them. When you look at their feedback, you will naturally let it sway yours. When you have your prep time, sit down with the manager form and fill out your review with a clear head. Go through the One on Ones you've had over the year to remember accomplishments and identify areas that need to be addressed.

SEND THE EMAIL OUT A MONTH IN ADVANCE

The more prep time, the better. There is no reason to spring this on your team one week before the year ends. I have a calendar reminder on October 15 so that I draft and send the email well in advance. As your organization grows, this process becomes more and more difficult to get ahead of. Help yourself out by setting reminders that keep you abreast of this annual activity.

CREATE A TRACKER

I'm a big fan of trackers. I highly recommend detailing the steps and people involved to standardize your performance review process across your business. That way, you'll have transparency into whether team members or managers are following through. From an HR standpoint, all of these documents need to be saved, so a tracker will give you all the data you need to ensure the proper documentation is in place.

WHAT CAN GO WRONG

There are a variety of things that can go wrong in the performance review process, especially when there's a lack of alignment and a performance issue that you need to address, so I want to prep you on a couple areas that you should look out for and how you should handle them.

LACK OF ALIGNMENT

This is the most obvious issue that can arise during a performance review. Your team member sees things one way and you see them another. This is where the preparation ahead of the review becomes incredibly beneficial. You should not be showing up to that review and be blindsided that your assessment drastically differs from the team member's. The reason the team members send their assessments a week ahead of time is to avoid these types of situations. In the prep process, after you've completed your assessment, review their assessment. When you determine that there isn't alignment, don't get defensive or upset. Look at the results. If you listed areas of opportunity that you *never* communicated when you look back in your One on One notes, whose fault is that? Yours. Not theirs. Equally, if they listed a strength that you listed as an opportunity, refer to their metrics in the One on Ones to determine if they did hit their results. There is no reason emotion should come in during this process. That's easier said than done, but the idea of structuring your organization with all of these touchpoints is to create clarity so that there aren't these massive gaps in expectations versus results. During the review, you need to be able to address the lack of alignment by using data. If you are wrong, I highly suggest you update your feedback. If they are wrong, bring the documentation so there is proof and not opinion in the conversation.

DEVELOPMENT PLAN IS OFF

What do you do when you've given feedback that was different from the team member's assessment of themselves and *then* the development plan comes back and it's not in alignment with the feedback that you gave? Yikes! This has happened on a handful of occasions in my reviews over the years and emphasizes why the development plan is so important. You might have said one thing in the review, but the team member could have taken the feedback in a different direction. That's why it's so critical for the team member to draft their own development plan based on what they heard and their next steps for development. *They* need to be bought into the plan, and it's a way for you to ensure that they heard the feedback you meant to give.

If the team member comes back with a plan that doesn't address the feedback, you pull back up the documentation from the performance review and discuss which areas are missing. I would use the Core Value of "alignment" to ground this conversation: "We said X in the meeting and agreed, but your plan only addresses Y. I was under the impression that we were aligned that X is the priority. Is there a reason you didn't include it in your development plan?"

I can't stress enough how much documentation really does help you. Without the forms, you have nothing to point back to when there are disagreements. This is especially the case when you have multiple managers and team issues arise. From an HR standpoint, it certainly protects you as well.

DEVELOPMENT PLAN TEMPLATE

AREAS OF DEVELOPMENT: Please share 4 – 6 areas based on Performance Review	ESTIMATED HOURS	QUARTER

CLIENT SUCCESS

"Before, our performance reviews were very by the book, checking off on a scale of one to ten how well they did in each area, never really focused on how they could improve in areas where they were struggling or had that opportunity, and nothing tied back to our Core Values. So we never really got that improvement or that guidance that we needed from the managers for our employees. There was no real structure to it. We checked the boxes, and we moved on.

So now with the new performance reviews, with our manager and our employees, we're able to structure those performance reviews so they align. We sit down, and we give the strengths for the employee and give the opportunities in each one of our Core Values. Then the employee has an opportunity to share their strengths and opportunities. Then, together, the employee and the manager create this development plan where they can be successful. It really feels like, for the first time, our employees have the opportunity to work with their managers to create this plan that's going to help them grow within the company, reach their success, and help them achieve their personal, professional, and financial goals. The feedback I've gotten from that is phenomenal. Everybody says it's the first time they've had an opportunity to express where they can improve. But we never put a negative spin on it. Everything is always positive, and I think that's what they appreciate. When Natalie uses the term 'opportunity' instead of 'weakness,' it creates that encouragement for the employees. I feel like our employees have more of a voice or an outlet to express their concerns in this format. We've been able to honestly retain some of our employees because of our performance reviews. They've been able to speak where they have concerns, and we've been able to address those because they feel that they finally have a platform to express those concerns and where we need to grow as a company, and then we can help them as an individual."

—TODD VOLLING, STRAY VOLTAGE

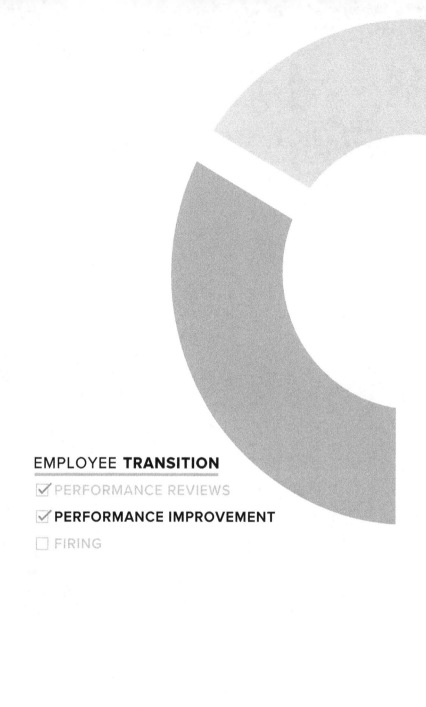

EMPLOYEE **TRANSITION**

- ☑ PERFORMANCE REVIEWS
- ☑ **PERFORMANCE IMPROVEMENT**
- ☐ FIRING

CHAPTER 15

PERFORMANCE IMPROVEMENT

This subject often gets tricky because you don't just fire somebody just because you don't like them. That's exactly the wrong way to do it. You do it because you've laid out a very specific process. And if they aren't willing to do the things necessary to fix their performance issues and you've made it so clear to them, that's why they leave. But not just because you on a whim one day make this decision.

Wouldn't it be great, though, if we could just hire dream team members who perfectly align with the Mission, the Vision, and the Values of the organization right off the bat? They overperform on their key performance indicators. They hit them every single time, and things just run smoothly. That would be awesome.

Unfortunately, that's not the world I have ever lived in, and I can promise you that it is not the world that you are going to live in as you build and grow your business. So the performance improvement process is setting up clear expectations with your team members for them to understand what happens if they do not hit the specified requirements. Now the word specify is important because as the business owner, as the leader, it is *your* responsibility to specify what the actual requirements are. The idea here is not to bring on a bunch of amazing team members to put all of this hard work into an interview process just for you not to fully give them the expectations and then get frustrated and mad that no one is able to read your mind. Nope. That's how an inexperienced business owner operates, and that's not you. You're going to make sure that you have metrics in place and that there's clarity.

But even if you provide those things, it is not 100 percent a given that team members will actually follow through on what you've established. So the performance improvement process really is your mechanism to be able to correct performance.

HOW TO THINK ABOUT PERFORMANCE IMPROVEMENT

The idea of improving performance is that your target is for the underperforming employee to continue to work in the business. Performance improvement is not some long-winded process for them to change as people and to go through some existential discovery on themselves. No, it's for them to meet the minimum requirement of their function within the business. It equally is not a place for you to already have made some foregone conclusion for you to use performance improvement as the mechanism for firing.

Let me make sure this is clear. When you go through a performance improvement process, the target is for the team members to *stay* with you. Long-term you do not wait to implement a performance improvement process until you are so fed up and frustrated, and there have been countless occurrences of the team member underperforming that you're just using it as a way for them to no longer be in the organization.

That's not the idea. When you first have an issue, you start to implement the process that I'm going to dive into.

WHY IT'S IMPORTANT

If team members don't have clarity on what the expectations are and they don't know what they need to do to improve their performance, your business, as it grows, will continue to have underperformers who don't know what next steps they need to take to fulfill the business requirements.

So in the improvement process, one of the best tips that I can give you is to put this in your employee handbook. The reason you put it in your handbook is that during onboarding, and linking out to the employee handbook, you're sharing all of the important policies and processes and resources that any new team member would need to know, but you're also sharing with them what the expectation is if they are no longer a fit.

It should clearly lay out the exact process for what happens if the team member doesn't hit their metrics. The employee handbook is such a critical element to this because without it you're just randomly and emotionally giving performance reviews and feedback.

I really leverage the One on One process and the handbook as the primary touchpoints to ensure that team members have full clarity about updates in their performance. When One on One coaching is not enough and the performance still is not hitting the minimum requirement, you just move into this next step of the process, which is a more serious coaching plan around fixing the behavior.

STEPS FOR PERFORMANCE IMPROVEMENT
STEP 1: TELL THEM

The first step of performance improvement is to tell the team member what they are doing incorrectly. It sounds simple, but by having the conversation and confronting the issue immediately, you are creating the best circumstances for a positive outcome.

How to Tell Them

Here is an example of how a team leader could communicate the need for improvement to a team member:

Leader: Hey, Joe! I noticed this morning that you came in at 8:40 instead of 8:30 and were late to our morning meeting. Per the handbook, our business opens at 8:30, and all team members need to be here on time to get organized for the priorities for the day. Why were you late?

Team Member: I hit traffic and didn't know that it was a hard start at 8:30.

Leader: Traffic happens to me too, so I leave fifteen minutes early to make sure it's not a problem. It's important everyone is here no later than 8:30 because our meeting creates alignment for the entire team and preps us to serve our clients. Can you make sure to get here on time moving forward?

Team Member: Absolutely.

Once you tell them and get their commitment, you're all good to go and you should move off it. Maybe they don't know that they're doing something wrong. Maybe they have not clearly ever been told that the expectation is X, Y, Z. That's why this whole performance improvement piece puts the initial onus on the business to have documented Policies and an Employee Handbook so that you can go through something that is very logical and doesn't bring emotions into it.

There is no way that your team members can read your mind, even the smallest of things that you think, *Oh, this would be so obvious*. The truth is: it doesn't matter that you think it's obvious. You need to have a place where you put those things in a written format so you can point to them and ensure there is no confusion or margin for "not knowing."

Vision, Commitment, and Execution

The Vision, Commitment, Execution (VCE) method was created to help individuals have more impactful conversations, especially hard conversations, when they matter the most. Sometimes when people try to communicate, they struggle with getting the context and purpose of the conversation across to the person they're speaking to. Keep in mind, this happens all the time in business, particularly because people are moving fast, they're under pressure, and they're trying to get as many things done as possible. This is when people tend to avoid the hard conversations. They put off any kind of interaction that could upset the workflow until a time where it's almost too late to bring clarity and intentionality to the forefront for a solution to their problem. Bad communication happens when someone dives straight into the execution steps. Starting a conversation by only talking about what's wrong without the larger context can feel like the right thing in the moment but is not effective when the goal is changing someone's behavior and getting their buy-in. It *is* important to address issues. But that's not where you start.

VCE is a simple communication framework designed to alleviate the stress, friction, and resistance of having hard conversations.

Vision

The Vision category is defined as the BIG PICTURE of what the business is trying to accomplish. What are you trying to accomplish in the next ten years? How are you trying to disrupt your industry? As an example, you could see Vision as a purpose to your customers, a purpose to your team, and even a purpose that speaks directly to you.

The idea behind starting with the Vision is being able to bring the conversation, especially difficult conversations, into context because here's the deal: if somebody is ten minutes late to work, is that really going to break the business? No, probably not. Nothing's going to be set on fire. There's going to be no massive issue. However, if the small things are overlooked, what confidence do you have that the bigger things are being followed through with? When you make it about something that's bigger than just the two people having the conversation, all of a sudden the emotion just goes away because if you're pointing fingers at somebody and getting on them, their natural response is to be defensive, and, even though that's okay, when somebody is defensive, you're not likely to have effective communication that gets the point across. So by putting in the Vision statement, you're able to remove the defensiveness from the team member. After you go into the Vision, the big why for this conversation, the next step is to go into commitment.

Commitment

The commitment category is the mutual commitment between two individuals to help one another achieve an overall goal. It could sound like, "This is what I'm going to commit to you, and this is what I need you to commit back to me." "Your commitment" means indicating what you're going to invest in or commit to in order to help them accomplish the change or the result that is required or being asked of them. "Their commitment" is your ask for the other person to do the things necessary to help you achieve the overall goals. With your role as a coach, it's important to share how you are specifically going to help make the change. This isn't to say that you'll be doing the work, but you will be involved and helping to get the behavior corrected.

Execution

The execution is the straightforward blocking and tackling for what needs to get done. It is the step-by-step plan for accomplishing the Vision. It's the "who, what, when, where, and how" plan. It can be broken down into three steps.

- Step 1 asks the question, "What needs to be done?" It's identifying the gaps between where you are now and where you want to be. From there, you identify the causes behind those gaps.
- Step 2 is about providing clear acknowledgment of what needs to be done and what you're willing to do. Recognize that if you or your team member is not willing to do something that is needed, the goal will not be accomplished.
- Finally, in Step 3, you need to determine the expected results. This is the tactical plan that will be used to execute on a daily, weekly, or monthly basis. It answers these questions:

What is the task? When it will be accomplished? And who is responsible for leading or completing it?

When you proactively utilize the VCE in preparation for having hard conversations, you're demonstrating true leadership, being fully self-aware and highly intentional. It's within these abilities where the magic of influence comes to fruition.

VERBAL WARNING FORM

VISION
Mission Statement:

Issue(s):

COMMITMENT
Team Member's Commitment:

Manager's Commitment:

If the Issue(s) persists, the next step will be a Performance Improvement Plan.

EXECUTION

EMPLOYEE'S SIGNATURE: _____ DATE: _____

MANAGER'S SIGNATURE: _____ DATE: _____

Now we move to the actual verbal warning. Once you've told them but the behavior still persists, a verbal warning must be issued with rapid speed. You do not wait. You don't pretend like it's not an issue. To build a high-performing culture, you need to address the issue ASAP, ideally on the same day. Let's break down this form.

Vision
Mission Statement

There are two parts of the Vision in the verbal warning documentation. The first is the Mission statement. Now, you could quite literally use your Mission statement that you created in Chapter 2, or you could tailor it to something that's more specific to the scenario.

Issue(s)

The second section is the Issues. Issues would include documenting the problem that you're having. So if the team member is only making fifty calls every day and they're supposed to be making sixty-five, right here is where you'd say the issue is not hitting the minimum metric. Again, this needs to be tied out to somewhere that you shared the expectation was sixty-five.

So processes have to be put in place, not only at first to establish that that's the baseline metric, but also for tracking how many calls they're actually making so that you can be looking at those numbers.

Commitment

Team Member's Commitment

The team member's commitment is going to be important because you're asking them to do a different behavior. So maybe this is going to be making the sixty-five calls. Maybe it's also going to be adding additional training and role-playing. Whatever you're expecting them to do to resolve the issue needs to be documented here.

Manager's Commitment

The leader is going to be responsible for ensuring that every single day, those calls are actually happening, listening to the calls so that they can provide coaching for any areas where there is an objection that the team member doesn't feel comfortable handling.

Whatever it is that the leader is going to do to help their team member become more successful is documented here.

This is putting the role of a coach into action and actually saying, "Okay, this is going to be my responsibility to help improve this. It's not just on you. I'm here to support you. I'm here to guide you. I've been here before and have gone through this. And so this is why I'm able to help you."

If the Issue(s) persist, the next step will be a performance improvement plan.

This statement is distinctly added to the commitment section. This is a game changer when it comes to identifying the seriousness of the situation. Where leaders go wrong in this exchange is they continue to say the same thing, the same thing, the same thing, but the team member, after so many times of you saying,

"Oh, you can't continue to be late," stops taking you seriously if you don't make it more serious. Once you put this in front of them and it's shared—that the next step will be a performance improvement plan—that adds gravity to the situation.

Ultimately it's up to them: are they willing to do what it's going to take to stay in this organization? Or are they not willing to do what it takes? By putting this statement in the commitment section and addressing it in the conversation during the verbal warning, you're setting the expectation that you are trying to make this work, that you are trying to help this team member out, and you're giving them every single tool that they need to be successful. *You're* committed to them. If they choose not to change their behavior and meet the expectations, the next step will be actually putting a legitimized plan in place. And if they do not do all of the specifics on that plan, the opportunity to work with you no longer exists.

Execution

The execution step is simply having them sign it and you signing it. This is to document that this conversation took place. You put the date on it, and this goes in their HR file. You also tell them that this goes into the HR file. After it's added to the HR file, it's the leader's responsibility to fulfill their commitment and hold the team member accountable to their commitment. Ideally, this solves the issue, and the team member goes back to being an excellent contributor to the business. If, however, the behavior persists, the last and final step is the performance improvement plan.

PERFORMANCE IMPROVEMENT PLAN FORM

VISION
Mission Statement:

Issue(s):

COMMITMENT
Team Member's Commitment:

Manager's Commitment:

EXECUTION

STEPS	MEASUREMENT	DATE

EMPLOYEE'S SIGNATURE: _____ DATE: _____

MANAGER'S SIGNATURE: _____ DATE: _____

It can be very disappointing when you move to a performance improvement plan because you're invested. You've now had two conversations, one of them documented, where you tried to help correct the behavior. When it gets to the performance improvement plan, you've already put in a significant amount of energy to fix the performance, but if the team member continues, for a third time, to not hit the target or to have bad behavior, this is the documentation that you will need to put the final plan in place before termination.

Vision and Commitment

The Vision and the commitment statements are the exact same as the verbal warning. The only need to modify would be if additional issues became problematic. If that's the case, you would add them to this form.

Execution

The biggest piece that is different from verbal warning to the performance improvement plan is the execution steps.

You'll notice on the form that there are distinct areas for steps, measurement, and dates.

The steps should be quantifiable action steps that the team member is responsible for taking. There should be no ambiguity in the steps. Depending on the situation, there could be as few as one and as many as ten distinct steps. I've never created a plan with more than ten steps.

When it comes to measurement, every step needs a defined method to determine if the step did or didn't happen. The date identifies the time period in which the behavior will be monitored. The dates determine the length of the performance improvement plan. I recommend that a plan is as condensed as possible and recommend to my clients to target two to four weeks. This can vary depending on the state you live in and the severity of the performance issue.

Let's use the instance of the team member being ten minutes late:

Step: Joe will show up by 8:30 every morning.

Measurement: Joe will clock in upon arrival and departure.

Date: four weeks

After this conversation takes place, both parties sign the document, and it should be added to the team member's HR file along with any additional support material. When it comes to the measurement methods, all records should be reviewed daily during the length of the performance improvement plan and added to the HR file for additional documentation. If there is an instance where the team member is late during the performance improvement plan, you need to start prepping for the termination process. If you've followed the above steps, the termination process should be painless. This is why having clear, documented conversations is important. In the moment, when you're juggling other things, documenting conversations can seem like meaningless paperwork, but I can assure you that you're protecting yourself and your organization.

The next part is never fun. I've fired hundreds of team members, and the conversations are never something I look forward to. But when you've laid out your expectations and followed the process in this chapter, and your team member has failed to meet the requirements of the performance improvement plan, you have no choice but to let the person go. It's what's best for you, them, your team, and your clients.

EMPLOYEE **TRANSITION**

- ☑ PERFORMANCE REVIEWS
- ☑ PERFORMANCE IMPROVEMENT
- ☑ **FIRING**

CHAPTER 16

FIRING

Here's the deal, guys. As a leader, the greatest gift you have chosen to give yourself is control of the people and the influences and the ideas in your environment.

That's why you start a business. You have this Vision, and you get to define how it's created and what it looks like. I've watched so many business owners give up their responsibility to truly lead their organizations because they allow other people to make decisions about *their* environment. But when you are in a business setting and you are in control of the ideas and the type of energy of that team and how you treat your customers, those decisions should be intentional. And when you're in that position, you have to take it seriously.

What I can assure you of is this: you will never create the perfect hiring system. Even after adopting the interview process I shared in Chapter 7, I can promise that you will make mistakes. To get to where you want to go, you need to confront that you will have to get rid of people because it will never be perfect. And that's okay because the target isn't 100 percent employee retention. The target is scaling your business and fulfilling your Mission.

People are not perfect. People will disappoint you. There will be bad employees. And you won't know at first because everybody puts on a great face in the interview, and they can kind of trick you. Or even worse, you didn't properly define and speak to them on your terms of what you're expecting. Regardless of why it happened, it's important to confront that firing team members will be a reality on your journey of scaling your business. So if we know that making hiring mistakes is inevitable, once you've identified that the team member isn't a fit, it's your responsibility to address the issue and not allow that person (or group of people) to suck the life out of you and your environment. You fire people for the sake of your team. You fire them for your clients' sake. And you fire them for your Mission's sake.

WHY I LOVE FIRING PEOPLE
CREATES CULTURE

Firing somebody allows you to define what the culture will and won't tolerate. When I look at the team members that I've let go, they weren't let go because we didn't like them. In most cases, I actually really enjoyed them. But they ultimately demonstrated that they were not in alignment with what was required to fulfill our Mission, which is to serve our clients.

So if there's somebody in the environment who is concerned with their title or that their idea is the one that's chosen and they're fighting and petitioning for that more than they are the needs and the concerns and the growth of our clients, that's not a fit for us. We want people who, at the end of the day, really understand that our Mission is to propel the people that we work with. And we don't let our liking for people determine whether somebody is a good fit for the business needs and the requirements that we have. When you let somebody go, you are showing every single person in your environment what is not tolerated.

ESTABLISHES STORIES

At your quarterly all-team meeting, you can say, "We don't want people who are self-serving" or "We believe in teamwork and collaboration," but the things that you say in those meetings are nowhere near as important as the things that you actually *do*. And those stories get perpetuated for years as you grow and scale your business and as it expands from five people to fifteen people to fifty people to two hundred people.

The examples that you create, especially early on in the business, about why somebody was let go will continue to be talked about ten years from now when you have two hundred employees. I can promise you that. So when you are thinking through that, it's not just for your environment today that you let a team member go: it's about the stories that are perpetuated that naturally create filters for the organization moving forward of what you will not tolerate. Because when a new hire joins and there are murmurs about what other team members have done to not be in alignment with the team or with the business, they will be talking about why certain people left.

That is why you should be letting the wrong person go. When you cut that cancer out, everyone understands that you're protecting your Core Values without you even saying it.

REMOVES NOISE

Firing a team member removes that noise you have as a leader or a business owner when you know that somebody is not living your Mission, your Vision, your Core Values and serving the people that you are committed to in your community or around the world. When you have noise, it lowers your confidence in what the business is able to do when you are dependent upon this person who isn't a fit to continue to be a part of what you're building.

When you start to lose confidence, you will put less energy and effort into serving your clients. You will start cutting corners. And it's just a natural process when you don't actually handle the things that you know you need to handle in business or in any area of your life. When you get lazy in one area, you start to be okay and start acquiescing to other areas where you're falling short. When it comes to a team member, if you haven't addressed the real issue and you allow this noise to exist, just know that you are actively deciding to decrease your confidence and to not fully go all out with pursuing that Mission and Vision that you set out for with the business early on.

Know that this is a choice. It's entirely up to you to get rid of your dependencies and figure out a way to scale. One of the things that remarkable leaders focus on most is doing things that are within the discipline and the accountability that they need in order to increase their confidence that they can wake up every single morning with every piece of tenacity they can muster and go charge the hill that day. And to the extent that you're not willing to just address the one team member and to go through the proper process to figure out if they should stay or if they should go, you're letting that go.

At my core, I'm the biggest pushover. I do not like having tough conversations. I do not like being confrontational. I'd prefer to let the little things go and not rock the boat. But I know that if I let one thing slip, I'm going to slip in other areas. And so I've had to learn through choosing to take a leadership role that I'm responsible to confront hard things. It does get easier, but it doesn't get any more fun. Just recently, I had to fire someone. It's easy to write "why I love firing people," but I don't want you to get the wrong impression with this. I was sick about it all day. My palms still get sweaty, and it was uncomfortable, but it's what's required of me to protect my environment and the goals of my team.

REMOVES THE FRICTION

Get people out of your environment who are not actually in alignment with you. Negative people, people who aren't willing to go all in, and people who are undermining you are cancerous to a business that is trying to grow. And cancer doesn't just stay in one area. It affects everything. It affects the marketing team. It affects the finance team. It affects the operations. It affects the sales. It affects your customers and clients and your reputation in the community. When you have one bad apple, the whole bunch is affected by that. When you refuse to remove it, you're acquiescing your goals and your team's goals because of your unwillingness to have a difficult conversation. And if you truly believe in your bones that what you are doing is a benefit to your community, to your clients, to your customers, to your patients, to whatever it is that you choose to serve, why would you allow that one person to be the thing that undermines all of that?

You have to kill the cancer. You have to just cut it out. Some people take the method of avoidance by saying, "Oh, well, they'll just, you know, eventually go because they're probably not happy." Well, why would you allow six months or three months or two weeks of damage to be done if you know that they're not the right fit? Gut up.

If you're feeling like it's an emotional decision (e.g., you're angry, mad, agitated), that's not the way you should be feeling nor is it the state you should be in during the conversation. You should know it's never fun. But the reason that I fire people is never around emotions. It's logical, and people self-select out of the opportunity because they weren't willing to do what it takes to achieve the targeted result.

HOW TO FIRE SOMEONE

Let's get real tactical here: you have a sales guy. Let's say the sales guy has been with you since the company first started, you met playing soccer, and you have now worked together for a decade.

For every salesperson, the minimum daily call requirement is 150 phone calls. But, you know, there's just "things that come up" and "conversations go longer," and you start hearing all sorts of excuses. You've known he's been slipping on his call volume for some time now, but this is the first month that sales are down. When you confront the numbers, you see that his call volume has dropped to seventy phone calls.

You sit down and have a conversation and say: "The minimum requirement of daily phone calls here is 150. That's the minimum. That's not rock star status. That's what is required to have this position, and you're currently not making the minimum. What impact do you think that has on the rest of the business?" He recognizes that this is an issue and commits to doing the

150. Then the next couple of weeks go by, and you see them slip back into that seventy.

You have two choices: take your business seriously or give up on your goals. This has nothing to do with him and everything to do with your ability to hold your environment accountable to the targets that you've set.

To the extent that you don't hold him accountable, you're actually making him a criminal. He does not feel good about the fact he's only making seventy calls now. He might give a bunch of excuses to justify it, but at the end of the day, he does not go home at night and feel good about living under his potential when he's done more in the past and is capable. If you are always firm and never wishy-washy about the target—if you never say, "It's okay to only do seventy"—I promise you he does not feel good about it.

When you're resolute about your Core Values of results and discipline and you leave it up to someone else to choose to either do what it takes or not, you've removed emotion from the conversation. All of the sudden, your ten-year history and old soccer days aren't what you're basing your decision on. He is choosing to not do what it takes if he continues to only make seventy calls. It's not a skill issue; it's not that you haven't trained him. He's just not willing to put the work in. You are doing him a favor by not continuing to set him up for failure.

And now you get to find somebody who is excited enough about the opportunity and their own potential to chase after the 150 and want to blow your mind with 200, because I promise you, there are people like that. Just because that one person that you've been with for a long time isn't willing to do it does not mean that you have to be dependent upon them or that everybody out there is like that.

CLIENT SUCCESS

"One individual that we hired wasn't performing at the levels we needed him to. We pulled him in and had discussions with him about how he's not performing and getting the results. He would respond with, 'Okay. Yup. I know. I'll change,' and literally the next week it was back to the same old, same old. We gave him a couple of chances, brought him in, and, then the last time, we basically took the format directly from Natalie and gave him a Verbal Warning, and then we gave him the Performance Improvement Plan, told him exactly how to do it, and how he was supposed to improve himself—still no results off of that. And then basically we went through the termination checklist at the very end.

We told him where he wasn't meeting up with our Core Values. He said, 'Yup, you're right. I still really want to work here.' I said, 'I realize that, but I need you to sign here, and we're going to have to move on.' It was very cordial. And I don't want to say it worked out great, but it worked out how it was supposed to. With the new process, we're able to walk through the process without hard feelings.

Everyone within this Cardone Ventures team that we've been able to surround ourselves with has been absolutely wonderful and encouraging for us. As business owners, a lot of times there's a lot of what I would call solitude and the component of being somewhat alone. To have that security and that network behind us is worth its weight in gold. We as humans are never going to be perfect, and we want to try to make things as good as possible for everyone. Especially as a caring business owner, I want everyone to be successful and have the opportunity to personally, professionally, and financially grow themselves. Since working with Cardone Ventures, our business is up 40 percent this year. It's been extremely eye opening and very humbling to be able to be within a network of people like that that think the way that we do.

—PAT AND TRISTA MORSTAD, PRECISION LANDSCAPE AND IRRIGATION

CONCLUSION

WHAT'S NEXT?

Now it's your time to implement. The greatest ideas in the world mean nothing without implementation. No matter where you're at in your business lifecycle, it is never too early or too late to develop a process for aligning, developing, and transitioning your team.

PEOPLE ESSENTIALS
WORKSHOP
WITH NATALIE DAWSON

☑ ALIGN YOUR TEAM

Craft your Mission, Vision, and Values

Attract and Hire Top Talent

Create Effective Onboarding Plans

☑ DEVELOP TOP PERFORMERS

Establish an Employee Maturity Model

Grow Top Talent

Duplicate Top Talent

☑ TRANSITION TALENT

Promote Talent

Create Performance Improvement Plans

Terminate Employees Effectively